24/6/2024

HERE ON EARTH

ATLAS

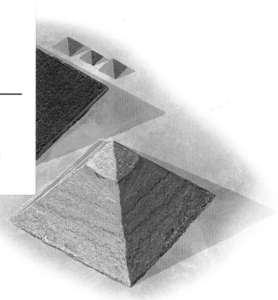

DK London
Senior editor Chris Hawkes
Senior art editor Rachael Grady
Editors Tom Booth, Anna Fischel, Anna Limerick
Designers David Ball, Chrissy Barnard, Mik Gates, Spencer Holbrook, Kit Lane
Illustrators Adam Benton, Stuart Jackon-Carter, Jon@kja-artists
Cartography Simon Mumford, Encompass Graphics

Jacket editor Claire Gell
Jacket designer Mark Cavanagh
Jacket design development manager Sophia MTT
Picture research Jayati Sood

Producer, pre-production Nadine King, Rob Dunn
Senior producer Gary Batchelor

Managing editor Francesca Baines
Managing art editor Philip Letsu
Publisher Andrew Macintyre
Publishing director Jonathan Metcalf
Associate publishing director Liz Wheeler
Art director Karen Self

First published in Great Britain in 2017
by Dorling Kindersley Limited
80 Strand, London WC2R 0RL

CONTENTS

Early Earth

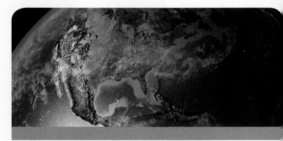

North America

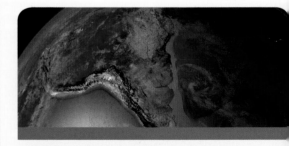

South America

Africa

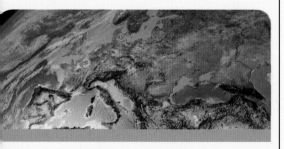

Europe

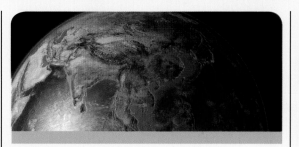

Asia

Australia and Oceania

Polar regions

The oceans

Reference

Kangaroo

The South Pole

EARLY EARTH

Under attack
Rock and debris from space crashed into Earth's surface during its early formation, turning it molten and triggering volcanic activity.

Early Earth

Earth's formation started shortly after the birth of the Sun, 4.6 billion years ago. A star exploding in nearby space caused a vast amount of interstellar dust to collapse in on itself. This formed our Sun, and over time the rest of the surrounding debris clumped together into planets. As these grew larger, their steadily increasing gravity pulled them into spheres. One of these was our planet, Earth, a rocky ball with a molten metal core, and a thin shell, called a crust, at its surface.

The layered interior structure of Earth emerged early in its evolution. Heat from Earth's molten core forced the crust, which is made up of large slabs of rock called tectonic plates, to move constantly. As these plates shunted around and crashed into each other, they caused earthquakes and fiery volcanoes, formed mountain ranges and entire continents, and helped create the conditions in which life could emerge.

This illustration shows the sequence of Earth's formation – from small fragments of rock and dust sticking together, to a planet with its own atmosphere.

Atmosphere
The air was heavy with carbon dioxide. Atmospheric pressure was higher than it is today, which allowed water to stay liquid at a far higher temperature than its modern boiling point.

Clouds
Clouds of water droplets could be seen in the sky, much as today.

First oceans
Liquid water, in which the first life formed, would have become permanent oceans at some time between 4.4 and 4.2 billion years ago.

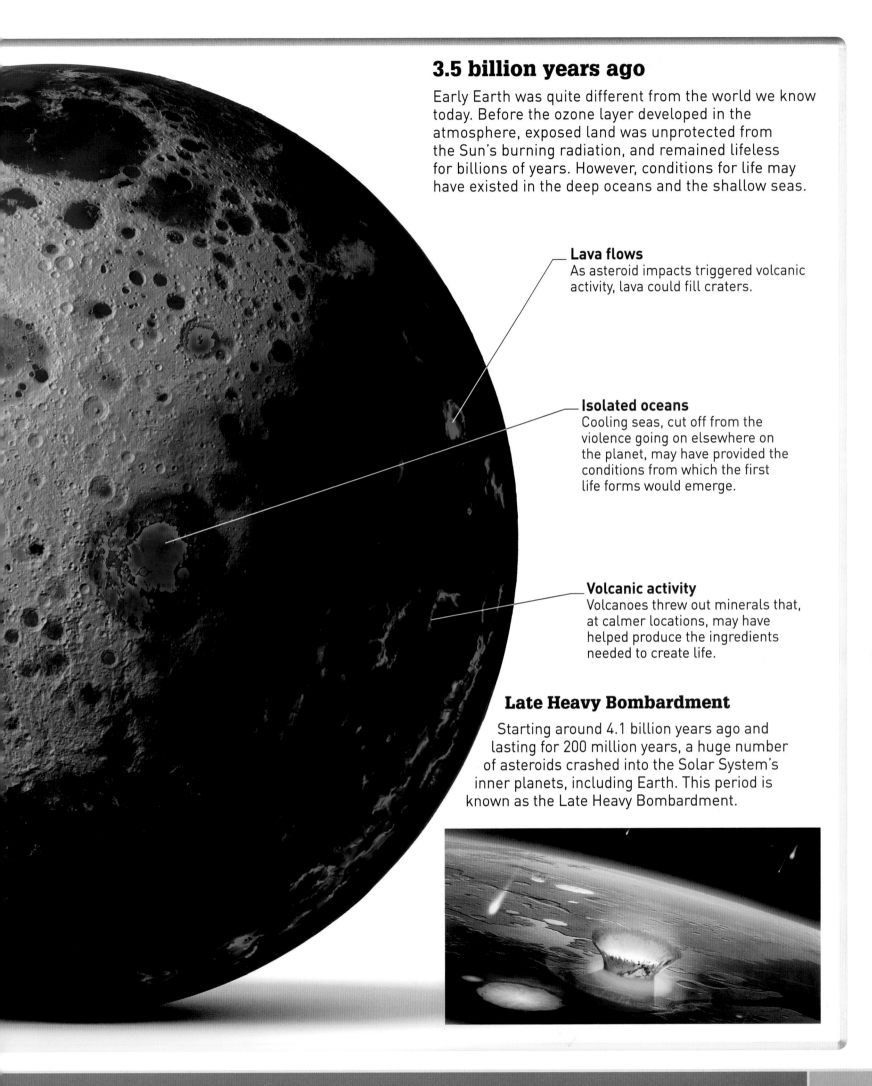

3.5 billion years ago

Early Earth was quite different from the world we know today. Before the ozone layer developed in the atmosphere, exposed land was unprotected from the Sun's burning radiation, and remained lifeless for billions of years. However, conditions for life may have existed in the deep oceans and the shallow seas.

Lava flows
As asteroid impacts triggered volcanic activity, lava could fill craters.

Isolated oceans
Cooling seas, cut off from the violence going on elsewhere on the planet, may have provided the conditions from which the first life forms would emerge.

Volcanic activity
Volcanoes threw out minerals that, at calmer locations, may have helped produce the ingredients needed to create life.

Late Heavy Bombardment

Starting around 4.1 billion years ago and lasting for 200 million years, a huge number of asteroids crashed into the Solar System's inner planets, including Earth. This period is known as the Late Heavy Bombardment.

BACTERIA, ARE THOUGHT TO HAVE EMERGED 3.5 BILLION YEARS AGO.

7

500 million years ago

By this stage of Earth's history two major continents had formed. The largest, Gondwana, was mainly tropical. Laurentia (now North America) had also drifted from the polar regions to the tropics and sat on the Equator. Temperatures were mild across the globe, but cooling.

In the water
Many life forms developed in the warm, shallow seas, including marine invertebrates such as *Hallucigenia*, a worm with limbs.

Hallucigenia

420 million years ago

Continents continued to shift. Avalonia (now split across present-day southern Britain and Canada) moved north to collide with Laurentia. Siberia headed north and Gondwana south, taking most of present-day Australia and Antarctica into the southern hemisphere. Sea levels started to rise.

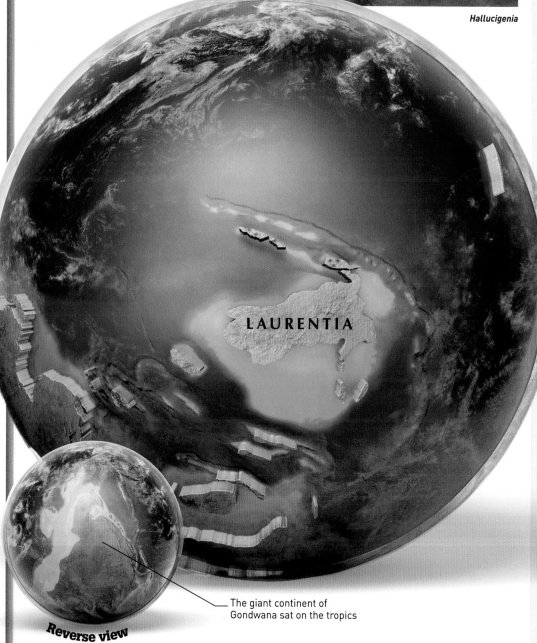

LAURENTIA

The giant continent of Gondwana sat on the tropics

Reverse view

LAURENT

Reverse view

Lifeless land
Carbon dioxide levels in the atmosphere were 15 times higher than today, and no animals could survive on land.

Early algae
There was no land vegetation, but many types of algae (plant-like oganisms that live in the sea) had appeared and diversified.

Animals
Millipedes, such as the one below, were the first known oxygen-breathing animals on land.

THE FIRST INSECTS ARE THOUGHT TO HAVE

In the water

The first coral reefs and fish appeared. *Guiyu oneiros* remains dating back to 419 million years ago have been found in Yunnan province, China.

Guiyu oneiros

380 million years ago

Laurentia and Baltica collided, closing up the Iapetus Ocean and forming the continent of Eurasia. The collision created the Appalachian-Caledonide Mountain Range, which extended from Scandinavia to the Appalachian Mountains in North America. Gondwana rotated clockwise, approaching Eurasia.

In the water

The "Age of Fish" saw a variety of lobe-finned fish and jawed predators. Placoderms (armoured fish) included the mighty *Dunkleosteus*.

Dunkleosteus

SIBERIA

BALTICA

GONDWANA

SIBERIA

EURASIA

GONDWANA

Reverse view

Plants

The tiny, but upright, *Cooksonia* was one of the first plants to colonize land. It was short, had branching stems, and lived in damp habitats.

Cooksonia

Fish with legs

The first tetrapods (four-legged animals) developed. The earliest were like fish with legs, such as *Ichthyostega*.

Ichthyostega

Archaeopteris

Plants

The landmasses turned green as woody, spore-bearing plants such as *Archaeopteris*, a treelike plant with ferny leaves, created major forests and swamps.

300 million years ago

By 300 million years ago, Eurasia had merged with Gondwana to form the supercontinent Pangea, which extended from high in the northern hemisphere to the South Pole, where ice caps spread. Siberia collided with eastern Europe, creating the Ural Mountains.

In the water
Fish and aquatic tetrapods, such as *Microbrachis* ("tiny limbs"), shared the seas with corals, crinoids (sea lilies), and brachiopods (molluscs).

Microbrachis

250 million years ago

All the continents were absorbed into the giant supercontinent Pangea. Global sea levels fell, while, in Siberia, massive volcanic eruptions poured out ash and gases, poisoning both the atmosphere and the oceans. Such events led to a global mass extinction.

SIBERIA

PANGEA

Reverse view

PANGEA

Reverse view

Animals
The shelled egg evolved, so tetrapods, such as *Ophiacodon*, could lay eggs on land without them drying out.

Ophiacodon

Plants
Lush swamps dominated by tree ferns laid the foundations for rich deposits of coal, and provided a habitat for arthropods, such as winged insects.

Animals
About 70 per cent of land species became extinct, including *Dimetrodo*

Dimetrodon

AROUND 250 MILLION YEARS AGO, A MASS EXTINCTION WIPED

Helicoprion

In the water
Falling sea levels exposed reefs. An estimated 95 per cent of marine species died out in the mass extinction – *Helicoprion* was one of the few survivors.

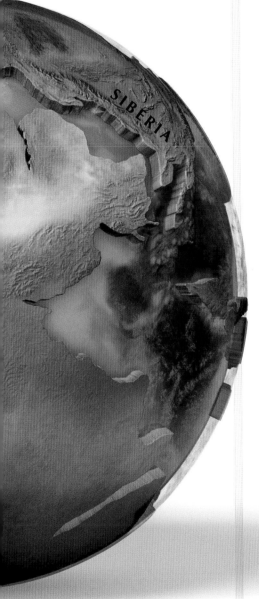
SIBERIA

220 million years ago
Pangea was at its largest – it extended from pole to pole – and sea levels had lowered. The supercontinent moved north, rotating anticlockwise. New life forms, including dinosaurs, started to evolve on the land.

In the water
Marine reptiles included turtles, frogs, crocodiles, and dolphin-like ichthyosaurs, such as *Mixosaurus*. Corals and molluscs also evolved new forms.

Mixosaurus

PANGEA

Reverse view

Plants
Half of all plant species died out. *Glossopteris*, widespread for 50 million years, declined, as did conifers, horsetails, and ferns.

Glossopteris

Animals
The first flies evolved, and early archosaurs (ruling reptiles), such as *Euparkeria*, paved the way for dinosaurs.

Euparkeria

Dicroidium

Plants
Vegetation adapted to the dry climate. Flora included conifers and the seed fern *Dicroidium*, which was distributed throughout Pangea.

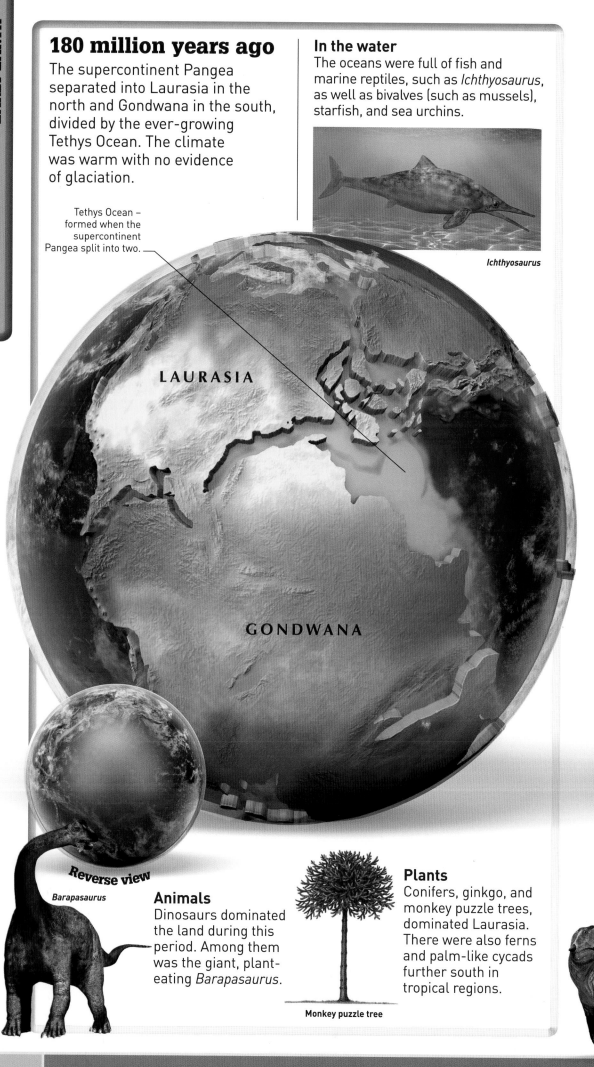

180 million years ago

The supercontinent Pangea separated into Laurasia in the north and Gondwana in the south, divided by the ever-growing Tethys Ocean. The climate was warm with no evidence of glaciation.

Tethys Ocean – formed when the supercontinent Pangea split into two.

In the water

The oceans were full of fish and marine reptiles, such as *Ichthyosaurus*, as well as bivalves (such as mussels), starfish, and sea urchins.

Ichthyosaurus

LAURASIA

GONDWANA

Reverse view

Barapasaurus

Animals

Dinosaurs dominated the land during this period. Among them was the giant, plant-eating *Barapasaurus*.

Plants

Conifers, ginkgo, and monkey puzzle trees, dominated Laurasia. There were also ferns and palm-like cycads further south in tropical regions.

Monkey puzzle tree

120 million years ago

Today's oceans began to take shape. The South Atlantic Ocean opened up as Africa and South America split apart, splintering Pangea further. North America was still attached to Europe, but India separated from western Australia and started to move in a northerly direction.

NORTH AMERICA

SOUTH AMERICA

Reverse view

Animals

Dinosaurs, such as *Psittacosaurus*, ruled the land. The first mammals and marsupials appeared, and birds filled the skies.

Psittacos...

MODERN-DAY MAMMAL GROUPS BEGAN TO

the water

chelon (giant sea turtles) and other
ea reptiles flourished. New species
strangely coiled creatures called
ammonoids thrived, as did sea
snails and anemones.

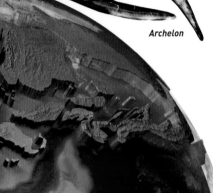

Archelon

80 million years ago

High sea levels flooded much of
North America and created a seaway
that extended from the Gulf of Mexico
to the newly forming Atlantic Ocean.
By 65 million years ago, India had
collided with Asia, causing volcanic
eruptions. An asteroid had hit Mexico,
causing a mass extinction.

In the water

New types of shellfish continued
to evolve and peculiar sea reptiles,
such as the long-necked
Albertonectes, came into being.

Albertonectes

AFRICA

India had split
from Africa.

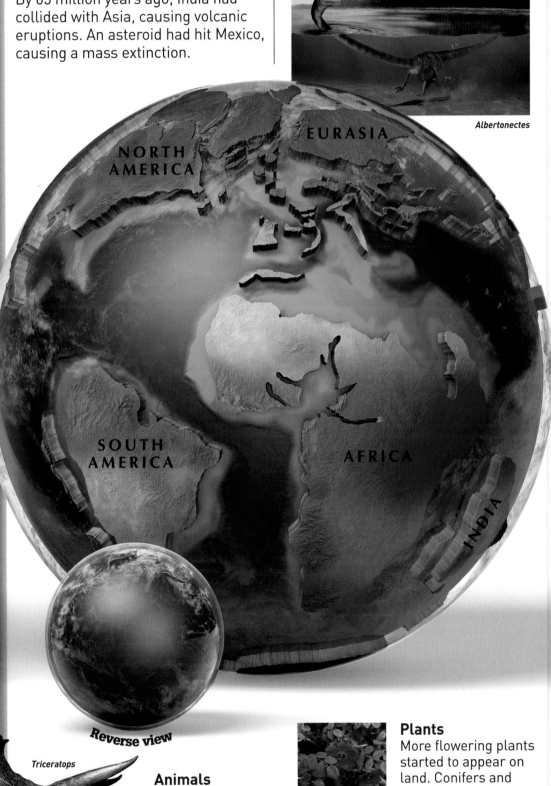

NORTH
AMERICA

EURASIA

SOUTH
AMERICA

AFRICA

INDIA

Reverse view

Plants

The first
angiosperms
(flowering plants),
such as magnolia,
colonized the land,
evolving alongside
pollinating insects,
including bees.

Triceratops

Animals

New dinosaurs
evolved, including
Triceratops. Snakes,
ants, and termites
also emerged.

Plants

More flowering plants
started to appear on
land. Conifers and
palm-like cycads
spread, thanks to
the success of their
seed-bearing cones.

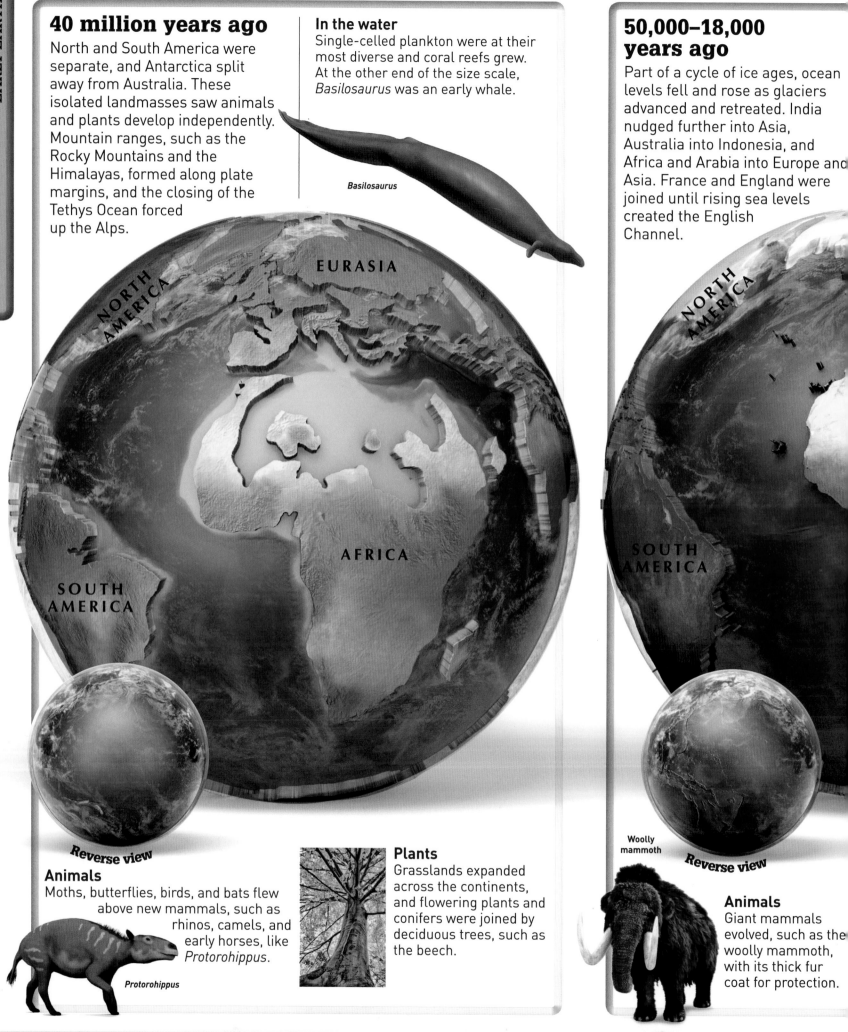

40 million years ago

North and South America were separate, and Antarctica split away from Australia. These isolated landmasses saw animals and plants develop independently. Mountain ranges, such as the Rocky Mountains and the Himalayas, formed along plate margins, and the closing of the Tethys Ocean forced up the Alps.

In the water

Single-celled plankton were at their most diverse and coral reefs grew. At the other end of the size scale, *Basilosaurus* was an early whale.

Basilosaurus

50,000–18,000 years ago

Part of a cycle of ice ages, ocean levels fell and rose as glaciers advanced and retreated. India nudged further into Asia, Australia into Indonesia, and Africa and Arabia into Europe and Asia. France and England were joined until rising sea levels created the English Channel.

NORTH AMERICA

EURASIA

AFRICA

SOUTH AMERICA

NORTH AMERICA

SOUTH AMERICA

Reverse view

Animals

Moths, butterflies, birds, and bats flew above new mammals, such as rhinos, camels, and early horses, like *Protorohippus*.

Protorohippus

Plants

Grasslands expanded across the continents, and flowering plants and conifers were joined by deciduous trees, such as the beech.

Woolly mammoth

Reverse view

Animals

Giant mammals evolved, such as the woolly mammoth, with its thick fur coat for protection.

THE OLDEST PAINTED CAVE ART - A RED DOT - WAS MADE

Bottlenose dolphin

the water
quatic mammals such as
olphins shared the seas with
ankton species that adapted
successive changes in the
ater temperature.

Present day

The last ice age ended and giant mammals became extinct around 12,000 years ago. By that time, humans had started to make their mark on the world. Human activity has triggered global warming and has affected natural cycles of glaciation. The consequences of this could have a major impact on life on Earth.

In the water

Coral reefs provide a habitat for up to a quarter of all marine species. Marine life is still diverse, with an estimated 2 million species living in the oceans.

Fish at coral reef

Reverse view

Plants

Steppe (grassland too dry for trees to grow) plant types expanded. Much land was tundra – so cold, dry, and windy, that only the hardiest plants grew.

Zebra

Animals

The land today is home to an estimated 6 million species of animal, including the zebra.

Plants

Tropical rainforests are home to about 40,000 known plant species, from tiny mosses to towering mahogany and kapok trees.

NORTH AMERICA

North America from space
North America is a huge continent that dominates the northern half of Earth's western hemisphere. From space, the Great Lakes and the Rocky Mountains are clearly visible.

North American Free Trade Agreement

Established in 1994, the North American Free Trade Association, also known as NAFTA, is an agreement signed by the United States, Canada, and Mexico. Its aim is to increase the flow of trade between the three countries.

ARCTIC OCEAN

Greenland
(to Denmark)

Ellesmere Island

Baffin Bay

Baffin Island

Alaska
The United States bought Alaska from Russia for $7.2 million in 1867.

Beaufort Sea

ASIA

NUNAVUT

Hudson Bay

ALASKA

YUKON

NORTHWEST TERRITORIES

MANITOBA

ONTAR

● Anchorage

CANADA

Bering Sea

ALBERTA   SASKATCHEWAN

Edmonton ●   Saskatoon ●   Winnipeg ●   MINNES

● Juneau

BRITISH COLUMBIA

Regina ●   NORTH DAKOTA

Gulf of Alaska

Calgary ●   Bismarck ●

Queen Charlotte Islands

Vancouver ●   MONTANA   SOUTH DAKOTA

Honolulu
HAWAII

Hawaiian Islands

PACIFIC OCEAN

Seattle ●   Helena ●   WYOMING   NEBRA

Hawaii
The volcanic Pacific islands became the United States' 50th state in 1959.

Vancouver Island

WASHINGTON

UNITED ST

Portland ●   IDAHO   Boise ●

United States of America
The United States is a country made up of 50 states.

OREGON

OF AMER

Denver ●

Salt Lake City ●   KAN

NEVADA   UTAH   COLORADO

Las Vegas ●   Albuquerque ●   NEW MEX

San Francisco ●   ARIZONA   Phoenix ●

CALIFORNIA

Los Angeles ●   El P

San Diego ●   Chihu

Tijuana ●

PACIFIC OCEAN

FAST FACTS

Total land area:
24,238,000 sq km
(9,358,340 sq miles)

Total population:
576 million

Number of countries: 23

Largest country:
Canada –
9,984,670 sq km
(3,855,103 sq miles)

Smallest country:
St Kitts and Nevis –
261 sq km (101 sq miles)

Largest country population:
United States of America –
321 million

NORTH AMERICA IS THE THIRD LARGEST AND THE FOURTH

Countries and borders

Greenland
Although part of Denmark, Greenland has been self-governing since 1979. It is the world's largest island.

The continent of North America is dominated by Canada, the second largest country in the world, and the United States of America, the richest. The seven countries of Central America have struggled with the problems of poverty and war in the past, but have experienced peace and economic recovery in recent years.

Canada
North America's largest country, Canada gained its independence from the United Kingdom in 1931 and has 10 provinces.

brador
Sea

NEWFOUNDLAND
AND LABRADOR

St John's

St Pierre & Miquelon (to France)

PRINCE EDWARD ISLAND

QUÉBEC

NEW BRUNSWICK

Halifax

NOVA SCOTIA

MAINE

Québec

Montréal

NEW HAMPSHIRE

VERMONT

Boston

OTTAWA

NEW YORK

MASSACHUSETTS
RHODE ISLAND
CONNECTICUT

Toronto

Philadelphia

New York

NEW JERSEY

PENNSYLVANIA

DELAWARE

Pittsburgh

MARYLAND

Detroit

WASHINGTON DC

MICHIGAN

WEST VIRGINIA

VIRGINIA

ONSIN

OHIO

WEST VIRGINIA

apolis

INDIANA

Raleigh

NORTH CAROLINA

Chicago

Indianapolis

ILLINOIS

KENTUCKY

SOUTH CAROLINA

A

Saint Louis

TENNESSEE

Atlanta

MISSOURI

GEORGIA

Kansas City

Jacksonville

Memphis

ALABAMA

S

ARKANSAS

MISSISSIPPI

FLORIDA

oma City

Miami

LAHOMA

LOUISIANA

New Orleans

Dallas

HAVANA

Houston

EXAS

US-Mexico border
This border is the most frequently crossed international border in the world.

San Antonio

Monterrey

Gulf of Mexico

Mérida

HONDURAS

BELIZE

MEXICO

BELMOPAN

TEGUCIGALPA

NICARAGUA

San Luis Potosí

GUATEMALA

MANAGUA

MEXICO CITY

Puebla

GUATEMALA CITY

SAN SALVADOR

SAN JOSÉ

iacán

Oaxaca

EL SALVADOR

COSTA RICA

Guadalajara

Acapulco

ATLANTIC OCEAN

KEY
- ● Capital city
- ● Major city

ST KITTS & NEVIS
Anguilla (to UK)

ANTIGUA & BARBUDA
Montserrat (to UK)
Guadeloupe (to France)
DOMINICA
Martinique (to France)

British Virgin Islands (to UK)

Virgin Islands (to US)

BRIDGETOWN
BARBADOS

Turks & Caicos Islands (to UK)

Puerto Rico (to US)

THE BAHAMAS

DOMINICAN REPUBLIC

ST LUCIA

ST. GEORGE'S
TRINIDAD & TOBAGO

ST VINCENT & THE GRENADINES

NASSAU

SANTO DOMINGO

PORT-OF-SPAIN

HAITI

GRENADA

Guantánamo Bay (to US)

PORT-AU-PRINCE

Curaçao (Neth.)

Bonaire (to Neth.)

CUBA

Navassa Island (to US)

Aruba (Neth.)

KINGSTON

JAMAICA

Cayman Islands (to UK)

Caribbean Sea

SOUTH AMERICA

PANAMA CITY

Dividing line
Panama's border with Colombia marks the divide between North and South America.

PANAMA

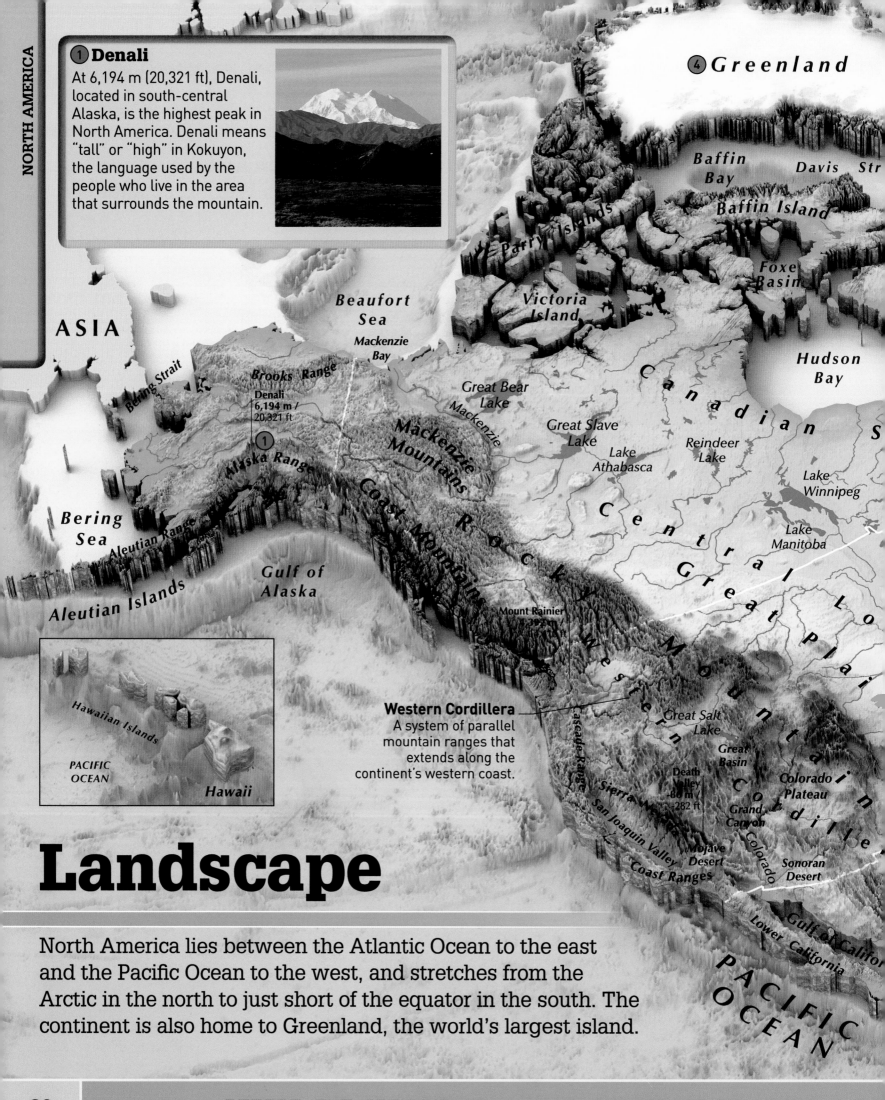

① Denali

At 6,194 m (20,321 ft), Denali, located in south-central Alaska, is the highest peak in North America. Denali means "tall" or "high" in Kokuyon, the language used by the people who live in the area that surrounds the mountain.

④ Greenland

ASIA

Baffin Bay

Davis Str

Baffin Island

Parry Islands

Foxe Basin

Victoria Island

Beaufort Sea

Mackenzie Bay

Hudson Bay

Bering Strait

Brooks Range

Denali 6,194 m / 20,321 ft

①

Great Bear Lake

Mackenzie

Canadian S

Alaska Range

Mackenzie Mountains

Great Slave Lake

Lake Athabasca

Reindeer Lake

Central

Lake Winnipeg

Bering Sea

Aleutian Range

Coast Mountains

Rocky Western

Lake Manitoba

Gulf of Alaska

Great Plai

Great Lo

Aleutian Islands

Mount Rainier

Western Cordillera
A system of parallel mountain ranges that extends along the continent's western coast.

Mountain Cordille

Cascade Range

Great Salt Lake

Hawaiian Islands

PACIFIC OCEAN

Hawaii

Sierra Nevada

Great Basin

Death Valley -86 m / -282 ft

Colorado Plateau

Grand Canyon

Colorado

San Joaquin Valley

Mojave Desert

Coast Ranges

Sonoran Desert

Lower California

Gulf of Californ

Landscape

North America lies between the Atlantic Ocean to the east and the Pacific Ocean to the west, and stretches from the Arctic in the north to just short of the equator in the south. The continent is also home to Greenland, the world's largest island.

PACIFIC OCEAN

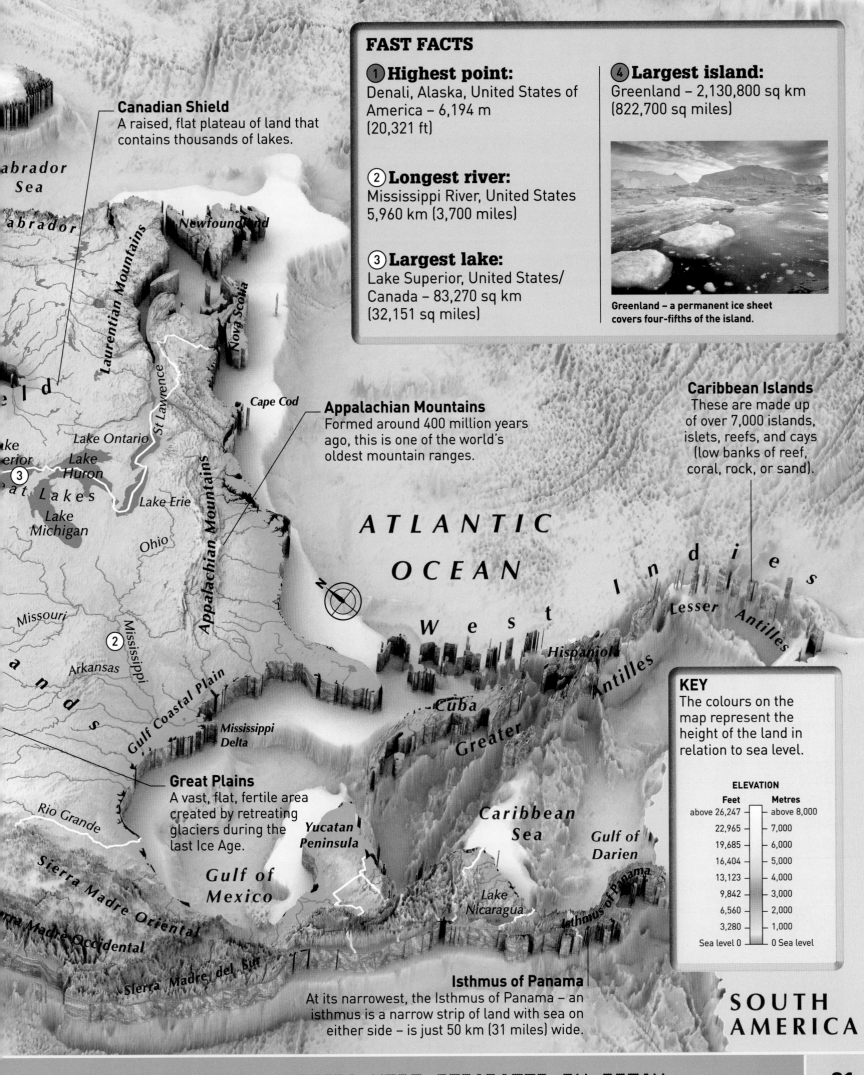

FAST FACTS

① Highest point:
Denali, Alaska, United States of America – 6,194 m (20,321 ft)

② Longest river:
Mississippi River, United States 5,960 km (3,700 miles)

③ Largest lake:
Lake Superior, United States/ Canada – 83,270 sq km (32,151 sq miles)

④ Largest island:
Greenland – 2,130,800 sq km (822,700 sq miles)

Greenland – a permanent ice sheet covers four-fifths of the island.

Canadian Shield
A raised, flat plateau of land that contains thousands of lakes.

Labrador Sea

abrador

Newfoundland

Laurentian Mountains

Nova Scotia

Cape Cod

Appalachian Mountains
Formed around 400 million years ago, this is one of the world's oldest mountain ranges.

Caribbean Islands
These are made up of over 7,000 islands, islets, reefs, and cays (low banks of reef, coral, rock, or sand).

St Lawrence

Lake Ontario

ke
erior

Lake Huron

Lake Erie

at Lakes

Lake Michigan

Ohio

Appalachian Mountains

ATLANTIC OCEAN

W e s t   I n d i e s

Lesser   Antilles

Missouri

Mississippi

Arkansas

Gulf Coastal Plain

Mississippi Delta

Hispaniola

Antilles

Cuba

Greater

KEY
The colours on the map represent the height of the land in relation to sea level.

Great Plains
A vast, flat, fertile area created by retreating glaciers during the last Ice Age.

Rio Grande

Yucatan Peninsula

Caribbean Sea

Gulf of Darien

Sierra Madre Oriental

Gulf of Mexico

Lake Nicaragua

Isthmus of Panama

erra Madre Occidental

Sierra Madre del Sur

Isthmus of Panama
At its narrowest, the Isthmus of Panama – an isthmus is a narrow strip of land with sea on either side – is just 50 km (31 miles) wide.

SOUTH AMERICA

ELEVATION	
Feet	**Metres**
above 26,247	above 8,000
22,965	7,000
19,685	6,000
16,404	5,000
13,123	4,000
9,842	3,000
6,560	2,000
3,280	1,000
Sea level 0	0 Sea level

Fascinating facts

Largest lake: **Lake Superior, United States/ Canada** – 83,270 sq km (32,151 sq miles)

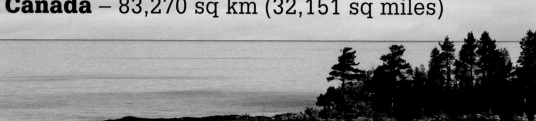

Deepest lake

Great Slave Lake, Canada –
614 m (2,014 ft) deep

Longest tunnels

Railway tunnel
Mount Macdonald Tunnel, British Columbia, Canada – 14.7 km (9.1 miles)

Metro line
Angrignon–Honoré-Beaugrand (Line 1 Green), Montreal Metro, Canada – 22.1 km (13.7 miles)

Road tunnel
Ted Williams Extension, Boston, United States – 4.2 km (2.6 miles)

Number of time zones 10

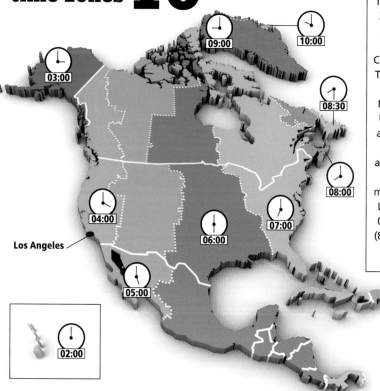

Los Angeles

12:00
The world is split into 39 time zones. Most are set whole hours ahead or behind Coordinated Universal Time (UCT) – the time at the Greenwich Meridian in London, UK. Some, however, are whole hours plus 30 or 45 minutes ahead or behind UCT. Therefore, on this map, if it was 12:00 in London, it would be 04:00 in Los Angeles (8 hours behind UCT).

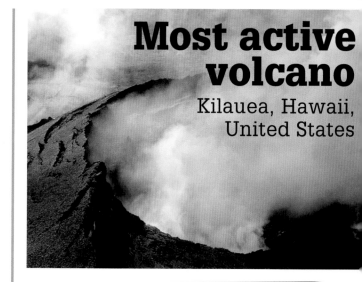

Most active volcano

Kilauea, Hawaii, United States

Official languages 7

Amerindian languages ▪ **Creole** ▪ Danish (Greenland) ▪ **Dutch** ▪ English ▪ **French** ▪ Spanish

Busiest airport

Hartsfield-Jackson Atlanta International Airport, Atlanta, US – **101,489,887 passengers per year**

Fastest train

North America's fastest train is the **Acela Express**, in the US, which can reach speeds of up to **240 km/h (150 mph)**

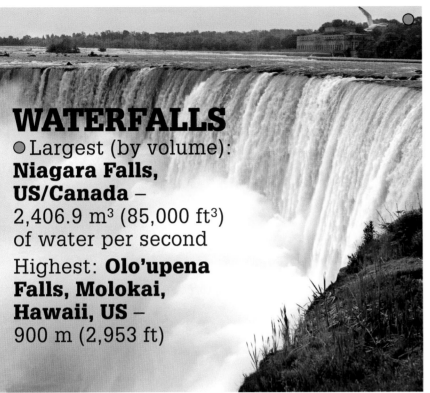

WATERFALLS

● Largest (by volume): **Niagara Falls, US/Canada** – 2,406.9 m³ (85,000 ft³) of water per second

Highest: **Olo'upena Falls, Molokai, Hawaii, US** – 900 m (2,953 ft)

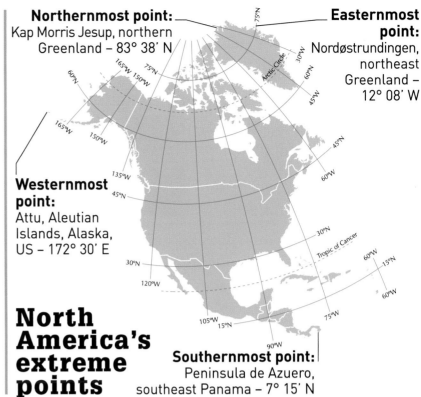

Northernmost point: Kap Morris Jesup, northern Greenland – 83° 38′ N

Easternmost point: Nordøstrundingen, northeast Greenland – 12° 08′ W

Westernmost point: Attu, Aleutian Islands, Alaska, US – 172° 30′ E

Southernmost point: Peninsula de Azuero, southeast Panama – 7° 15′ N

North America's extreme points

Longest coastline

Canada – **202,080 km (125,567 miles)**

Longest bridge

Lake Pontchartrain Causeway, Louisiana, USA – **38.442 km (23.89 miles)**

Highest bridge

Royal Gorge Bridge, Colorado, USA – **291 m (955 ft)**

BIGGEST GLACIER Bering Glacier, Alaska, US

Tallest buildings

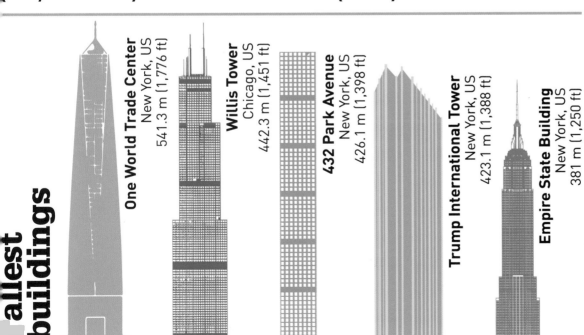

One World Trade Center New York, US 541.3 m (1,776 ft)

Willis Tower Chicago, US 442.3 m (1,451 ft)

432 Park Avenue New York, US 426.1 m (1,398 ft)

Trump International Tower New York, US 423.1 m (1,388 ft)

Empire State Building New York, US 381 m (1,250 ft)

Most visited cities (Visitors per year)

New York, US 12.27 million

Los Angeles, US 5.2 million

Miami, US 4.52 million

Toronto, Canada 4.18 million

Vancouver, Canada 3.76 million

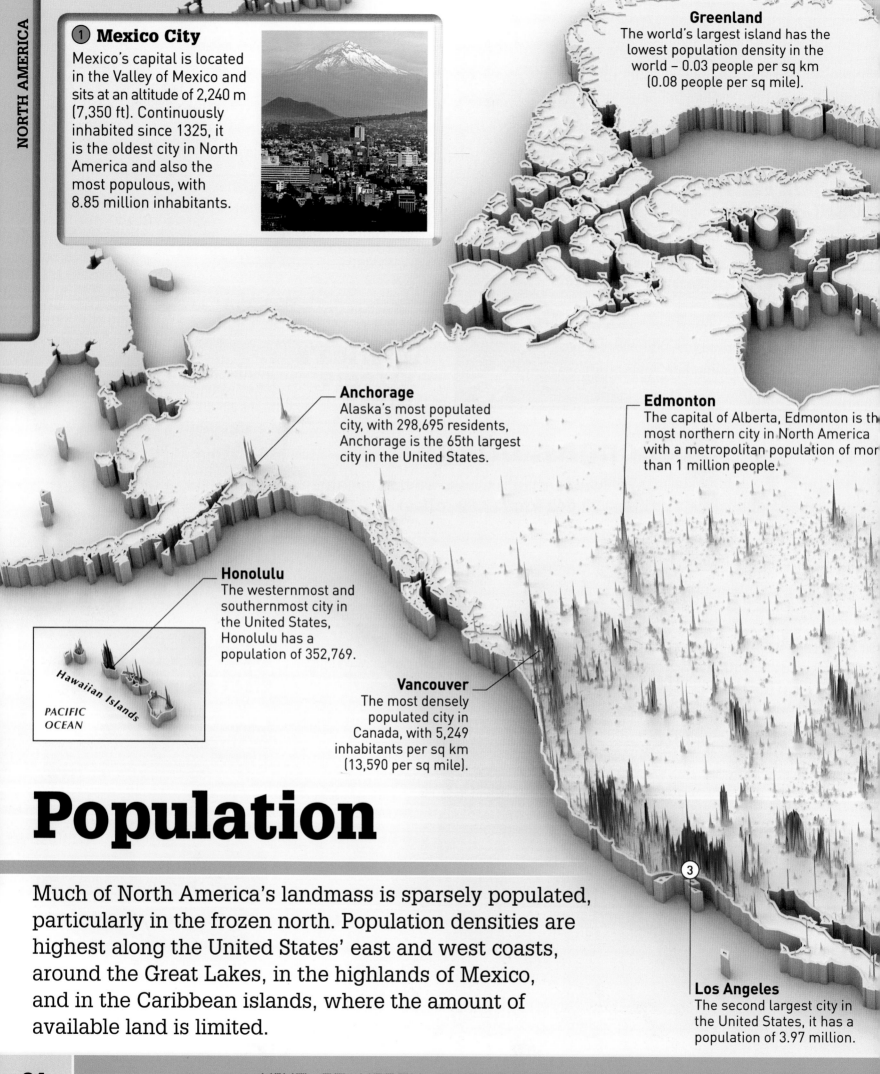

① Mexico City

Mexico's capital is located in the Valley of Mexico and sits at an altitude of 2,240 m (7,350 ft). Continuously inhabited since 1325, it is the oldest city in North America and also the most populous, with 8.85 million inhabitants.

Greenland
The world's largest island has the lowest population density in the world – 0.03 people per sq km (0.08 people per sq mile).

Anchorage
Alaska's most populated city, with 298,695 residents, Anchorage is the 65th largest city in the United States.

Edmonton
The capital of Alberta, Edmonton is the most northern city in North America with a metropolitan population of more than 1 million people.

Honolulu
The westernmost and southernmost city in the United States, Honolulu has a population of 352,769.

Hawaiian Islands

PACIFIC OCEAN

Vancouver
The most densely populated city in Canada, with 5,249 inhabitants per sq km (13,590 per sq mile).

Population

Much of North America's landmass is sparsely populated, particularly in the frozen north. Population densities are highest along the United States' east and west coasts, around the Great Lakes, in the highlands of Mexico, and in the Caribbean islands, where the amount of available land is limited.

Los Angeles
The second largest city in the United States, it has a population of 3.97 million.

NINE OF NORTH AMERICA'S 10 MOST DENSELY POPULATED

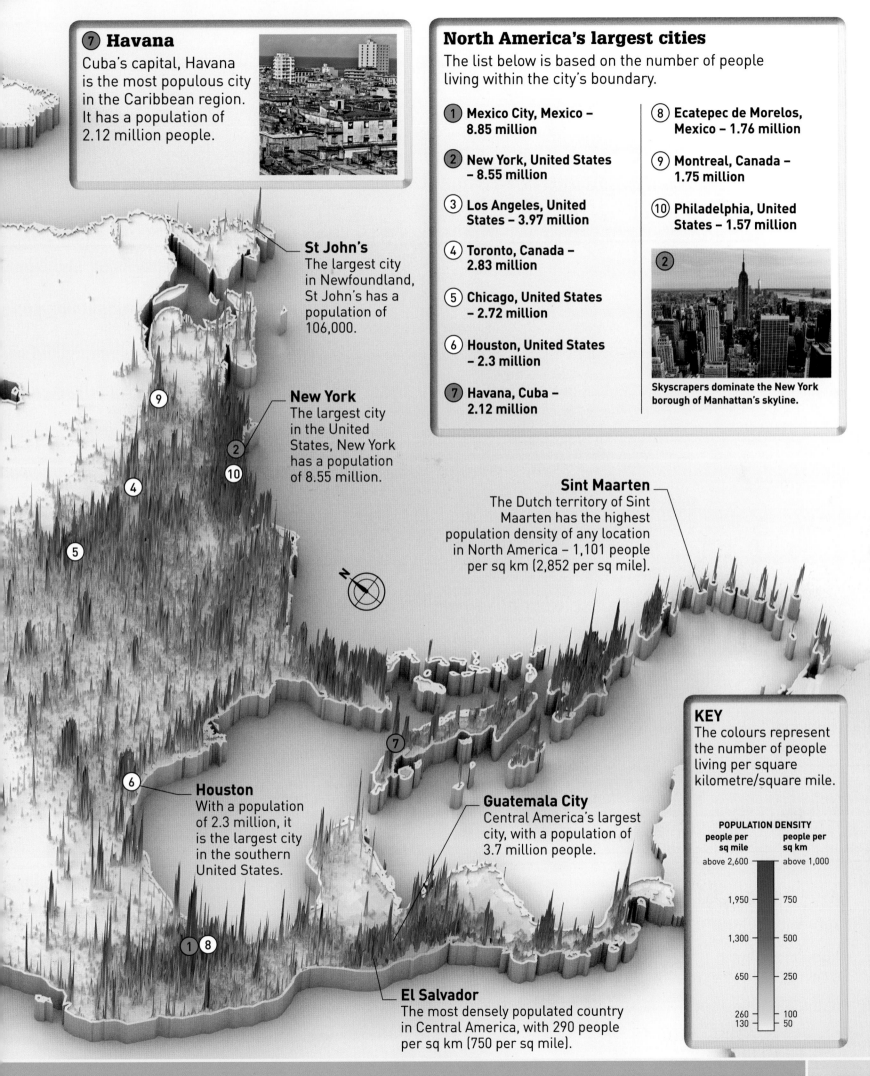

⑦ Havana

Cuba's capital, Havana is the most populous city in the Caribbean region. It has a population of 2.12 million people.

North America's largest cities

The list below is based on the number of people living within the city's boundary.

① **Mexico City, Mexico** – 8.85 million

② **New York, United States** – 8.55 million

③ **Los Angeles, United States** – 3.97 million

④ **Toronto, Canada** – 2.83 million

⑤ **Chicago, United States** – 2.72 million

⑥ **Houston, United States** – 2.3 million

⑦ **Havana, Cuba** – 2.12 million

⑧ **Ecatepec de Morelos, Mexico** – 1.76 million

⑨ **Montreal, Canada** – 1.75 million

⑩ **Philadelphia, United States** – 1.57 million

Skyscrapers dominate the New York borough of Manhattan's skyline.

St John's

The largest city in Newfoundland, St John's has a population of 106,000.

New York

The largest city in the United States, New York has a population of 8.55 million.

Sint Maarten

The Dutch territory of Sint Maarten has the highest population density of any location in North America – 1,101 people per sq km (2,852 per sq mile).

Houston

With a population of 2.3 million, it is the largest city in the southern United States.

Guatemala City

Central America's largest city, with a population of 3.7 million people.

El Salvador

The most densely populated country in Central America, with 290 people per sq km (750 per sq mile).

KEY

The colours represent the number of people living per square kilometre/square mile.

POPULATION DENSITY

people per sq mile	people per sq km
above 2,600	above 1,000
1,950	750
1,300	500
650	250
260	100
130	50

The Grand Canyon

Formed over millions of years by the flow of the Colorado River, the Grand Canyon is a steep-sided canyon in the state of Arizona, United States. It is 446 km (277 miles) long, 29 km (18 miles) wide at its widest point, and reaches a depth of 1,857 m (6,093 ft).

Granite Gorge
The most-visited section of the Grand Canyon, it is the starting point for the majority of rafting trips through the canyon along the Colorado River.

Gran

G r a n d   C a n y o n

Grand Canyon Village

Grand Canyon Lodge

Colorado River

Bright Angel Canyon

Walhalla Plateau

Cape Royal

Granite Gorge

Desert View

Colorado River

P a i n t e

South Rim
Approximately 90 per cent of tourists catch their first dramatic glimpse of the Grand Canyon from here.

Painted Desert
Starting at the eastern edge of the Grand Canyon, the Painted Desert is 19,425 sq km (7,500 sq miles). It is named for its multi-coloured layers of rock, which range from grey to purple, and from orange to pink.

THE FIRST EUROPEAN TO SEE THE GRAND CANYON WAS GARCIA

Tuckup Canyon
A 160-km (100-mile) long trail route on the North Rim of the Grand Canyon.

Tuckup Canyon

Colorado River

Great Thumb Mesa

Powell Plateau

Kanab Plateau

Grand Canyon Village
Occupied since the 1800s, Grand Canyon Village was originally built around the terminus for the Grand Canyon Railway, which brought tourists to the area.

North Rim
Temperatures on the North Rim are usually lower than those found at the South Rim because it is 300 m (1,000 ft) higher.

Kaibab Plateau
Reaching an elevation of 2,817 m (9,200 ft), this heavily forested plateau contrasts sharply with the arid lowlands to its south.

*K a i b a b
P l a t e a u*

C o c k s c o m b

Cockscomb
A trail area running to the north of the Grand Canyon, its highest point is Cockscomb Rock at 1,527 m (5,009 ft).

Kaibab National Forest
A 670,000-hectare (1.6 million-acre) forest that borders both the north and south of the Grand Canyon.

M a r b l e   C a n y o n

Desert

Colorado River
From its source in the Rocky Mountains, the Colorado River flows for 2,330 km (1,450 miles) and passes through Mexico before emptying into the Gulf of California.

Marble Canyon
This marks the beginning of the Grand Canyon. Despite its name, the canyon contains no marble – it gets its name from the colour of its limestone walls, which resemble the colour of marble.

○ Chichen Itza

The largest and most famous Mayan site, Chichen Itza, Mexico, was a major urban centre between 750 and 1200 CE. The highlight of the site is the El Castillo pyramid, whose four sides are made up of 365 steps (one for each day of the solar year).

Illulisat Icefjord ─

Located 350 km (220 miles) north of the Arctic Circle, the area's many icebergs have made Illulisat a popular tourist destination.

Illulisat Icefjord,
Greenland

Mount Shishaldin,
Alaska,
United States

Mount Shishaldin

The highest mountain peak on the Aleutian Islands (2,857 m/9,373 ft), Mount Shishaldin is the most symmetrical cone-shaped volcano on Earth.

The Bow,
Calgary,
Canada

Mount Rushmore,
South Dakota,
United States

Ninstints,
British Columbia,
Canada

○ **Old Faithful,**
Wyoming, United States

Space Needle,
Seattle, United States

Mauna Loa,
Hawaii, United States

Hawaiian Islands

PACIFIC OCEAN

Redwood National Park,
California, United States

Golden Gate Bridge

When it opened in 1937, it had the longest main span (1,280 m/4,200 ft) of any suspension bridge in the world.

Hoover Dam,
Nevada-Arizona,
United States

Golden Gate Bridge,
San Francisco,
United States

Chaco Canyo[n]
New Mexico,
United State[s]

HOLLYWOOD

Hollywood Sign,
Los Angeles,
United States

The **United States** is the world's **second-** most-visited country.

KEY
○ **Landmark location**

Famous landmarks

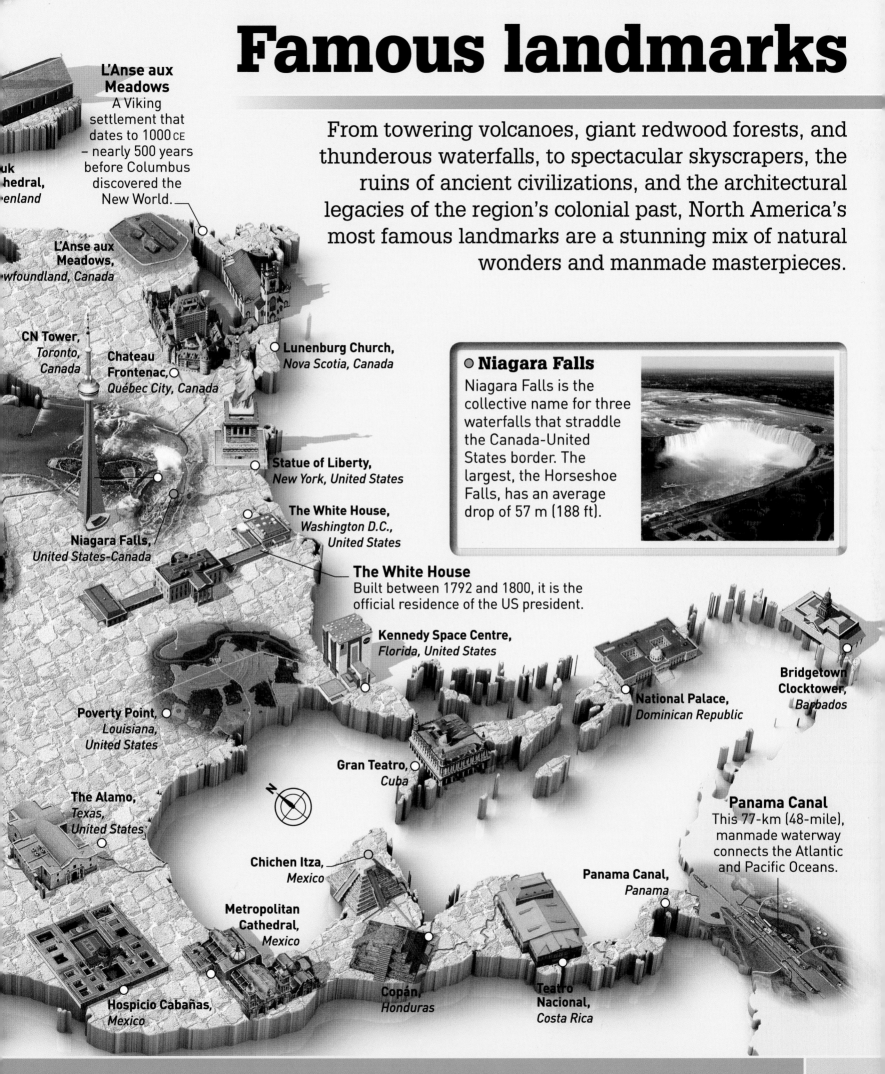

L'Anse aux Meadows
A Viking settlement that dates to 1000 CE – nearly 500 years before Columbus discovered the New World.

uk
hedral,
enland

L'Anse aux Meadows,
wfoundland, Canada

CN Tower,
Toronto, Canada

Chateau Frontenac,
Québec City, Canada

Lunenburg Church,
Nova Scotia, Canada

Statue of Liberty,
New York, United States

Niagara Falls,
United States-Canada

The White House,
Washington D.C., United States

From towering volcanoes, giant redwood forests, and thunderous waterfalls, to spectacular skyscrapers, the ruins of ancient civilizations, and the architectural legacies of the region's colonial past, North America's most famous landmarks are a stunning mix of natural wonders and manmade masterpieces.

◉ Niagara Falls
Niagara Falls is the collective name for three waterfalls that straddle the Canada-United States border. The largest, the Horseshoe Falls, has an average drop of 57 m (188 ft).

The White House
Built between 1792 and 1800, it is the official residence of the US president.

Kennedy Space Centre,
Florida, United States

Poverty Point,
Louisiana, United States

National Palace,
Dominican Republic

Bridgetown Clocktower,
Barbados

Gran Teatro,
Cuba

The Alamo,
Texas, United States

Panama Canal
This 77-km (48-mile), manmade waterway connects the Atlantic and Pacific Oceans.

Chichen Itza,
Mexico

Panama Canal,
Panama

Metropolitan Cathedral,
Mexico

Hospicio Cabañas,
Mexico

Copán,
Honduras

Teatro Nacional,
Costa Rica

☻ Tornado Alley

Tornado Alley is a nickname given to an area in the southern United States that experiences a high number of tornadoes. A tornado is a column of air that spins at high speed while maintaining contact with both the ground and the storm clouds above.

EISMITTE
0 10

RESOLUTE
0 9

IQALUIT
0 6

Coldest inhabited place

Prospect Creek Camp, in Alaska, is the coldest inhabited place in North America. On 23 January 1971, the thermometer there tumbled to -62.2°C (-80°F).

COPPERMINE
0 9

CHURCHILL
3 9

ANCHORAGE
3 8

FORT VERMILION
1 10

WINNIPEG
5 10

Lowest

The lowest temperature ever recorded in North America is -63°C (-81.4°F) at Snag, Yukon, in Canada, on 3 February 1947.

CALGARY
5 12

SIOUX CITY
5 12

VANCOUVER
3 10

Wettest

Henderson Lake, British Columbia, Canada, received an average of 7 m (276 in) of rain and snow when measurements were taken between 1923 to 1935 and 1998 to 2000.

BOISE
4 14

DENVER
7 11

HONOLULU
7 10

Hawaiian Islands

PACIFIC OCEAN

Highest

The highest temperature ever recorded in North America is 56.7°C (134°F) in Death Valley, California, United States, on 10 July 1913.

LAS VEGAS
8 13

SAN FRANCISCO
5 10

Climate

LOS ANGELES
7 11

GUAYMAS
7 9

The climate in North America ranges from freezing Arctic conditions in the far north to desert in the southwest, and tropical conditions in Florida, Central America, and the Caribbean. Central and southern regions are prone to severe storms, including hurricanes and tornadoes.

Driest

Batagues in Baja California, Mexico, is the driest place in North America. It receives just 30.5 mm (1.2 in) of rain per year.

IN 1998-99, A WORLD RECORD 2,896 CM (1,140 IN) OF SNOW FELL

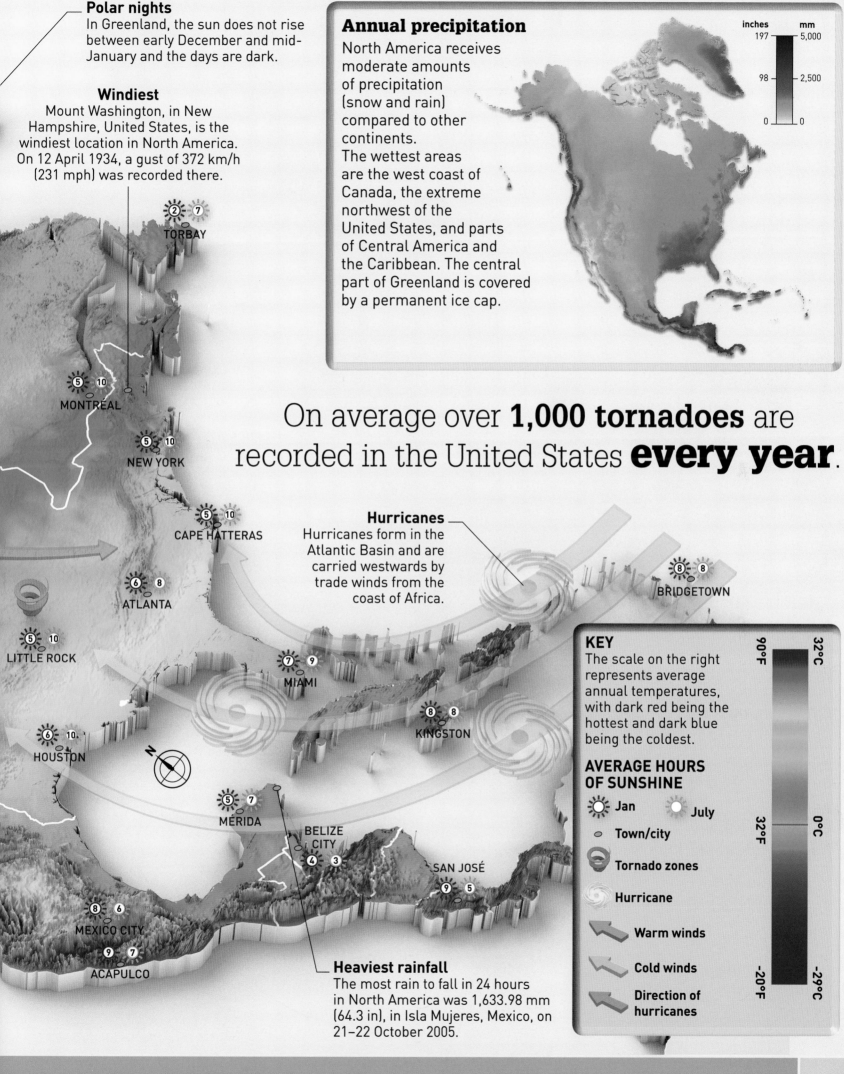

Polar nights
In Greenland, the sun does not rise between early December and mid-January and the days are dark.

Windiest
Mount Washington, in New Hampshire, United States, is the windiest location in North America. On 12 April 1934, a gust of 372 km/h (231 mph) was recorded there.

Annual precipitation
North America receives moderate amounts of precipitation (snow and rain) compared to other continents.
The wettest areas are the west coast of Canada, the extreme northwest of the United States, and parts of Central America and the Caribbean. The central part of Greenland is covered by a permanent ice cap.

inches / mm
197 — 5,000
98 — 2,500
0 — 0

② ⑦
TORBAY

⑤ ⑩
MONTRÉAL

⑤ ⑩
NEW YORK

⑤ ⑩
CAPE HATTERAS

⑥ ⑧
ATLANTA

⑤ ⑩
LITTLE ROCK

⑥ ⑩
HOUSTON

⑦ ⑨
MIAMI

⑧ ⑧
KINGSTON

⑧ ⑧
BRIDGETOWN

⑤ ⑦
MÉRIDA

BELIZE CITY
④ ③

SAN JOSÉ
⑨ ⑤

⑧ ⑥
MEXICO CITY

⑨ ⑦
ACAPULCO

On average over **1,000 tornadoes** are recorded in the United States **every year**.

Hurricanes
Hurricanes form in the Atlantic Basin and are carried westwards by trade winds from the coast of Africa.

KEY
The scale on the right represents average annual temperatures, with dark red being the hottest and dark blue being the coldest.

90°F — 32°C
32°F — 0°C
-20°F — -29°C

AVERAGE HOURS OF SUNSHINE
☀ Jan   ○ July
◯ Town/city
🌀 Tornado zones
🌀 Hurricane
➤ Warm winds
➤ Cold winds
➤ Direction of hurricanes

Heaviest rainfall
The most rain to fall in 24 hours in North America was 1,633.98 mm (64.3 in), in Isla Mujeres, Mexico, on 21–22 October 2005.

BIOMES

North America has a number of different biomes – large geographical areas of distinctive plant and animal groups – from deciduous forests in the south to tundra in the far north.

- Ice
- Tundra
- Boreal forest/Taiga
- Temperate coniferous forest
- Temperate broadleaf forest
- Temperate grassland
- Mediterranean
- Tropical coniferous forest
- Tropical broadleaf forest
- Tropical dry broadleaf forest
- Tropical, sub-tropical grassland
- Desert
- Flooded grassland
- Mangrove

Walrus
This mammal uses its tusks to haul its enormous 1,500 kg (3,000 lb) body out of the water.

Harbour sea
This common se slows its heartb when swimmin underwater.

Musk ox
Gets its name from the strong odour males emit during the rutting season.

Ringed seal
This seal can hold its breath underwater for 45 minutes.

Snowy owl
An unusual owl because it hunts by day.

American black bear
Short, non-retractable claw make it an excell tree-climber.

American bison
North America's largest land mammal, it can weigh up to 1,000 kg (2,205 lb).

Antelope
The fastest land animal in North America, the antelope can reach speeds of 88.5 km/h (55 mph).

Elk
Male elk clash antlers in batt for mating righ

Arctic ground squirrel
This squirrel doubles its weight during summer to prepare for a seven-month hibernation.

Steller sea lion
The largest sea lion species. Male bulls can be 1,000 kg (2,205 lb).

Dall sheep
This sheep has thick, curled horns that stop growing in the winter.

Grey wolf
Wolf pairs can track prey for up to 80 km (50 miles).

Coyote
A nocturnal canine that will eat whatever it finds.

Hawaiian Islands

PACIFIC OCEAN

Hawaiian monk seal
The only species of seal native to Hawaii. It is highly endangered.

Striped skunk
This mammal's foul-smelling oil can be smelt up to 1.6 km (1 mile) away.

Great white shark
A streamlined swimmer with powerful jaws that contain seven rows of knifelike teeth.

Golden eagle
North America's largest bird of prey can reach speeds of 320 km/h (200 mph) in a vertical dive.

Bighorn sheep
The horns of a male can weigh more than its whole skeleton.

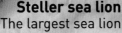

Wildlife

A diverse array of animals roams North America's lands and waters. The contrasting biomes – from freezing tundra in the north to tropical rainforest in the south – provide a remarkable range of habitats for countless species to survive and thrive.

Grey seal
Two fur layers and blubber help this seal keep warm in freezing water.

Starnosed mole
Nose tentacles help this mole identify food.

Raccoon
Dextrous front paws help this mammal snatch fish from rivers and pick snacks from bins.

River otter
Webbed feet and sleek body make this playful mammal an excellent swimmer.

Beaver
Powerful jaws help this rodent fell trees and build dams in deep water.

Rattlesnake
Highly venomous, this snake grows new "rattle" segments when it sheds its skin.

Prairie dog
A rodent that lives in underground towns on grasslands.

American alligator
This extremely territorial and powerful predator can be 4 m (13 ft) long.

● Oldest and largest
Situated above a dormant (inactive) volcano, and boasting more than half of the world's great geysers, Yellowstone, in Wyoming, United States, became the world's first national park in 1872. This has helped preserve the landscape from human exploitation, and protect its animal herds from poachers.

Lemon shark
A stocky shark that lives in groups in tropical coastal waters.

Magnificent frigatebird
An agile flier with long wings and a forked tail.

Caribbean reef shark
This shark lives on reefs, and can dive to 380 m (1,250 ft).

Olive Ridley sea turtle
A solitary, open-ocean dweller; females return to land to lay eggs.

American crocodile
The largest crocodile species, it lives in brackish (slightly salty) water.

ARACHNIDS (SPIDERS AND SCORPIONS), 914 BIRDS, AND 662 REPTILES.

Canada
Despite its vast size (only the Russian Federation is larger), almost 90 per cent of Canada is uninhabitable. The cold temperatures in the country's frozen north are too extreme for humans to live there.

Hawaii
With 953,000 people, O'ahu is the most populous of Hawaii's main islands.

PACIFIC
OCEAN

Hawaiian Islands

California
The Los Angeles-Long Beach-Anaheim area is the most densely populated region in the United States.

By night

This image of North America at night provides a fascinating insight into where people live. The major urban areas are found in the eastern half of the United States, California, and central Mexico, but much of the northern half of the continent is uninhabited.

OF THE 50 STATES THAT MAKE UP THE UNITED STATES,

Greenland
This vast island has only 13 towns with a population of more than 1,000 people. The largest is Nuuk, which has a population of 16,500.

Canada
An estimated 90 per cent of Canada's population live within 160 km (100 miles) of the US border.

Great Lakes
Towns and cities frame the shores of the Great Lakes, which are clearly visible in this image.

Caribbean islands
Although some of North America's most densely populated territories can be found in the Caribbean region, some of the islands are also home to ever-growing rural populations.

● **Cayman Islands** – Along with Anguilla, Bermuda, and Sint Maarten, this is one of four North American territories with an entirely urban population.

● **Haiti** – A consequence of the devastating 2010 earthquake, the number of people living in towns increased by 3.78 per cent between 2010 and 2015.

● **Montserrat** – Only 9 per cent of this volcanic island's population live in an urban environment.

● **Trinidad and Tobago** – Fewer people live in towns here than anywhere else in North America.

District of Columbia
Over 600,000 people live in an area of just 177 sq km (68 sq miles).

Mexico
Over half the country's 123.2 million population live in a small band of land in the centre of the country.

KEY
Illuminated areas on the map reflect urban, built-up areas and roads, in contrast to rural regions.

█ **Rural area**

▓ **Urban area**

Costa Rica
Has an urban population of 76.8 per cent – the highest in Central America.

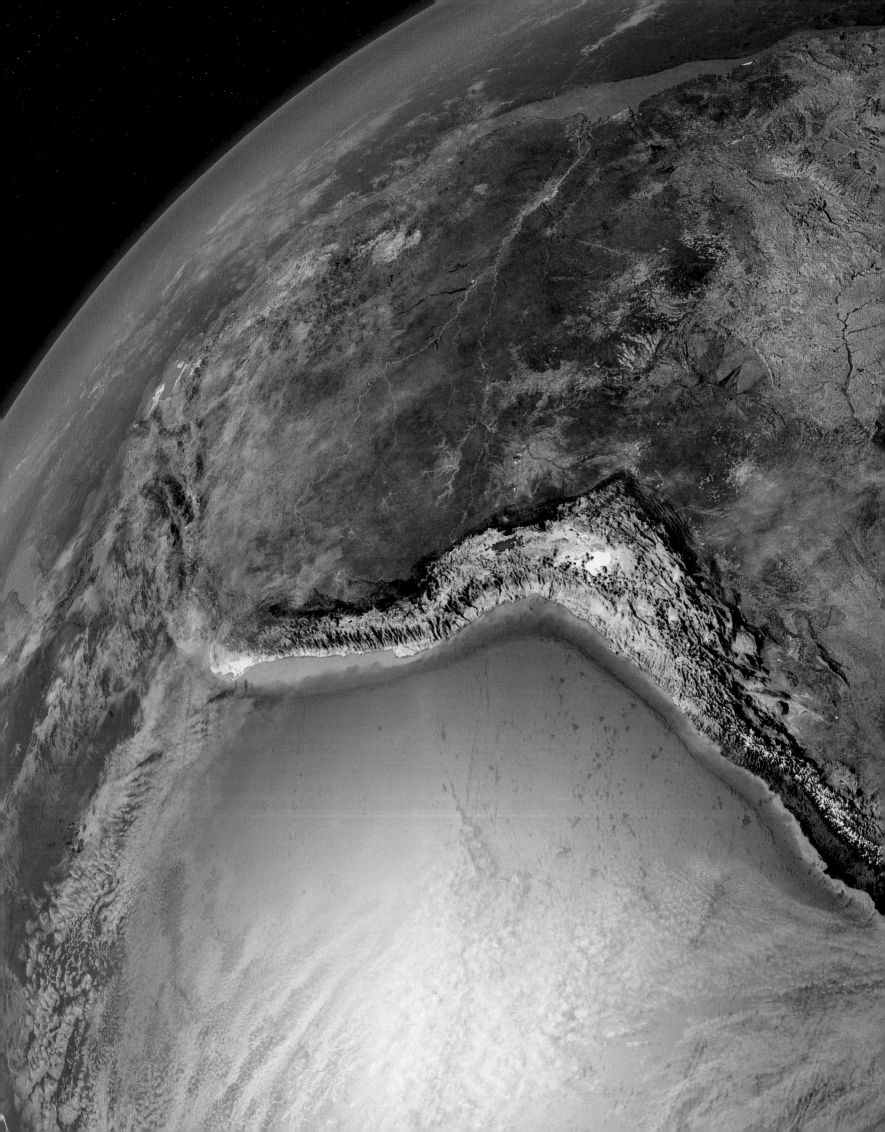

SOUTH AMERICA

Mountains and forests
The Andes mountain range and the mighty Amazon rainforest dominate South America, which runs from the Caribbean Sea in the north to the Tierra del Fuego in the south.

ATLANTIC OCEAN

Venezuela
Venezuela has the largest oil reserves in South America, and the oil industry is crucial to the country's economy.

French Guiana
The only remaining colony on the South American mainland, French Guiana is governed by France.

CAYENNE

PARAMARIBO

GEORGETOWN

French Guiana (to France)

GUYANA SURINAME

Cumaná

Santaré

Caribbean Sea

Maracay **CARACAS**

VENEZUELA

Maracaibo

Manaus

Cartagena

COLOMBIA

Gulf of Darien

Medellín **BOGOTÁ**

Porto Velho

NORTH AMERICA

Gulf of Panama

Cali

Rio Branco

Colombia
For 11 years following its independence from Spain in 1819, Colombia also included the territories of Venezuela and Ecuador.

Iquitos

QUITO

ECUADOR

Guayaquil

B O

LA PA

PERU

Cusco

Galápagos Islands (to Ecuador)

Trujillo

PACIFIC OCEAN

Callao **LIMA**

Arequipa

Ari

Peru
The Inca Empire covered much of the territory of modern Peru. It was overthrown by Spanish soldiers led by Francisco Pizarro in 1533.

Simón Bolívar
Popularly known as "the Liberator", Simón Bolívar (1783–1830) was a Venezuelan military leader who played a major role in the continent's uprising against the Spanish Empire. His ideas – and dream of creating a united continent – continue to inspire many South Americans even today.

Countries and borders

For centuries, most of South America was under Spanish or Portuguese rule. Although the majority of countries became independent in the early 19th century, the languages and cultures of their past rulers have shaped the lives of people living there today.

CHILE AND ECUADOR ARE THE ONLY SOUTH AMERICAN

Brazil
The Treaty of Tordesillas, signed in 1494, divided South America between Spain and Portugal. The Portuguese were given the lands to the east that would one day become Brazil.

FAST FACTS

Total land area:
17,840,000 sq km
(6,890,000 sq miles)

Total population:
410 million

Number of countries: 12

Largest country:
Brazil – 8,515,770 sq km
(3,287,957 sq miles)

Smallest country:
Suriname – 163,820 sq km
(63,251 sq miles)

Largest country population:
Brazil – 204.3 million

The Brazilian city of Rio de Janeiro is home to the world's biggest carnival.

Fortaleza
Natal
Recife
São Luís
Belém
Salvador
Palmas de Tocantins
B R A Z I L
Vitória
BRASÍLIA
Belo Horizonte
Goiânia
Rio de Janeiro
Cuiabá
Campinas
São Paulo
Campo Grande
Curitiba
Santa Cruz
A
oamba
UCRE
PARAGUAY
ASUNCIÓN
Ciudad del Este
Porto Alegre
Resistencia
URUGUAY
Salta
A
Santa Fe
MONTEVIDEO
ntofagasta
R
Rosario
C
Córdoba
BUENOS AIRES
La Plata
Bolivia
amed after
imón Bolívar,
olivia became
n independent
epublic in 1825.

G
Mendoza
Bahía Blanca
E
SANTIAGO
Valparaíso
N
T
Chile
Bernardo O'Higgins and José de San Martín were the revolutionaries who led Chile to independence in 1818. Today, they are two of the country's greatest national heroes.

I
Puerto Montt
N
A

A T L A N T I C

O C E A N

Falkland Islands
The islands are a self-governing British colony. In 1982, Argentina invaded, leading to a brief, but bloody, war.

STANLEY

Falkland Islands
(to UK)

Punta Arenas

KEY
● Capital city   ● Major city

The Orinoco
This river flows in a vast arc through Venezuela, passing through the flat Llanos, where it creates vast floodplains during the rainy season.

Guiana Highlands
The tablelike mountains of the Guiana Highlands are surrounded by cliffs that rise up to 400 m (1,300 ft).

ATLANTI

Tumuc-Humac Mountains

Pakaraima Mountains

Guiana Highlands

Branco

Amazon

Represa Balbina

Rio Negro

Caribbean Sea

Punta Gallinas

Orinoco

Lake Maracaibo

Llanos

Japurá

Amazon

Madeira

Gulf of Darien

Cordillera Oriental

Magdalena

Cauca

Cordillera Central

Cordillera Occidental

Putumayo

Amazon Basin

Purus

Juruá

Gulf of Panama

Cordillera Real

Chimborazo
6,310 m / 20,702 ft

Amazon

The Colombian Andes
The Andes separate into three ranges in Colombia. Two of the country's great rivers, the Río Magdalena and the Río Cauca, have their sources here.

Nevado Huascarán
6,768 m / 22,205 ft

Marañón

Ucayali

Andes

Lake Titicaca

Altip

Gulf of Guayaquil

Punta Negra

The Altiplano
The second highest plain in the world, the Altiplano, in Bolivia, has an average altitude of 3,750 m (12,303 ft).

Galápagos Islands
This isolated group of volcanic islands is home to a number of unique animal species.

Galápagos Islands

The Andes
Spanning 7,000 km (4,300 miles) along the western side of South America, the Andes is the longest mountain range on Earth.

PACIFIC OCEAN

Landscape

South America boasts an extraordinary range of landscapes, from the tropical forests on the northern coast to the icy fjords of Tierra del Fuego. The Andes mountains extend along the west coast, while the Amazon Basin dominates the heart of the continent. To the south lie the grasslands of the Pampas.

③ Lake Titicaca
South America's largest lake, Lake Titicaca is the highest navigable body of water in the world, with an elevation of 3,800 m (12,500 ft). It is home to the Uros people, who live on floating islands made from reeds. One island even houses a meeting hall and a school.

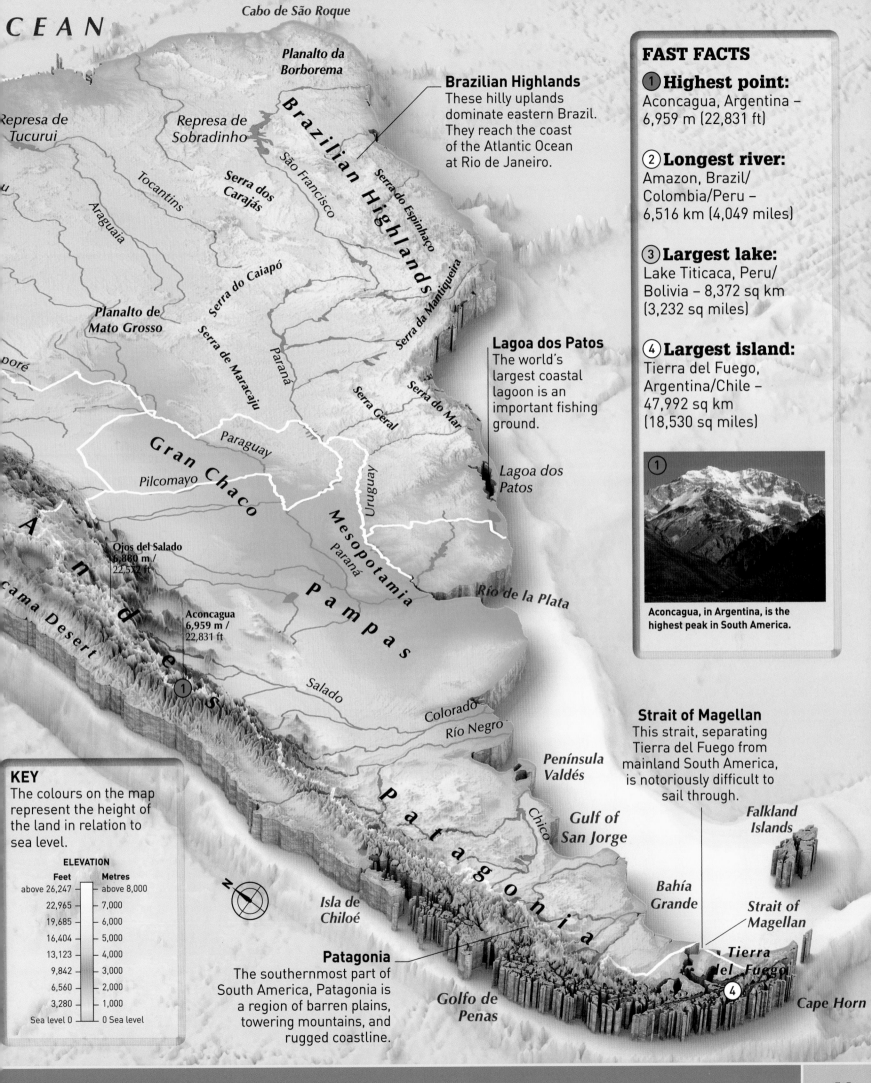

O C E A N

Cabo de São Roque

Planalto da Borborema

Brazilian Highlands
These hilly uplands dominate eastern Brazil. They reach the coast of the Atlantic Ocean at Rio de Janeiro.

Represa de Tucurui

Represa de Sobradinho

Tocantins

Araguaia

Brazilian Highlands

Serra dos Carajás

Serra do Espinhaço

São Francisco

poré

Planalto de Mato Grosso

Serra de Maracaju

Serra do Caiapó

Paraná

Serra da Mantiqueira

Serra Geral

Serra do Mar

Gran Chaco

Paraguay

Pilcomayo

Uruguay

Mesopotamia

Paraná

Lagoa dos Patos
The world's largest coastal lagoon is an important fishing ground.

Lagoa dos Patos

A n d e s

Ojos del Salado
6,880 m / 22,572 ft

Pampas

Aconcagua
6,959 m / 22,831 ft
①

Río de la Plata

cama Desert

Salado

Colorado

Río Negro

Península Valdés

Chico

Gulf of San Jorge

Strait of Magellan
This strait, separating Tierra del Fuego from mainland South America, is notoriously difficult to sail through.

Falkland Islands

KEY
The colours on the map represent the height of the land in relation to sea level.

P a t a g o n i a

Isla de Chiloé

Bahía Grande

Strait of Magellan

ELEVATION

Feet	Metres
above 26,247	above 8,000
22,965	7,000
19,685	6,000
16,404	5,000
13,123	4,000
9,842	3,000
6,560	2,000
3,280	1,000
Sea level 0	0 Sea level

Patagonia
The southernmost part of South America, Patagonia is a region of barren plains, towering mountains, and rugged coastline.

Golfo de Penas

Tierra del Fuego

④

Cape Horn

FAST FACTS

① **Highest point:**
Aconcagua, Argentina – 6,959 m (22,831 ft)

② **Longest river:**
Amazon, Brazil/Colombia/Peru – 6,516 km (4,049 miles)

③ **Largest lake:**
Lake Titicaca, Peru/Bolivia – 8,372 sq km (3,232 sq miles)

④ **Largest island:**
Tierra del Fuego, Argentina/Chile – 47,992 sq km (18,530 sq miles)

①

Aconcagua, in Argentina, is the highest peak in South America.

Fascinating facts

BIGGEST GLACIER

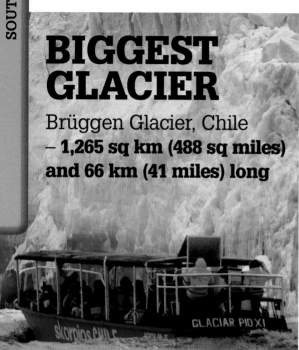

Brüggen Glacier, Chile – **1,265 sq km (488 sq miles) and 66 km (41 miles) long**

Number of time zones 4

Rio de Janeiro

 The world is split into 39 time zones. Most are set whole hours ahead or behind Coordinated Universal Time (UCT) – the time at the Greenwich Meridian in London, UK. Some, however, are whole hours plus 30 or 45 minutes ahead or behind UCT. Therefore, on this map, if it was 12:00 in London, it would be 09:00 in Rio de Janeiro, Brazil (3 hours behind UCT).

COUNTRY WITH THE MOST NEIGHBOURS

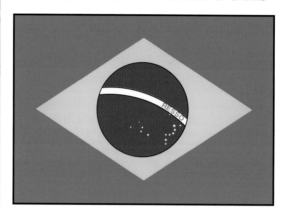

Brazil (10)

French Guiana, **Suriname,** Guyana, **Venezuela,** Colombia, **Peru,** Bolivia, **Paraguay,** Argentina, **Uruguay**

Longest tunnels

Railway tunnel
Cuajone–El Sargento tunnel, Peru – 14.72 km (9.1 miles)

Road tunnel
Fernando Gomez Martinez tunnel, Colombia – 4.6 km (2.86 miles)

Number of official languages 5

Portuguese ▪ Spanish ▪ English ▪ Dutch ▪ French

Longest coastline
 Brazil – **7,491 km (4,655 miles)**

Most active volcano
Villarrica, Chile

 **Busiest airport**

Biggest airport São Paulo-Guarulhos Airport, Brazil – passengers in 2015: **35.96 million**

Highest:
Angel Falls, Venezuela – 979 m (3,212 ft)

Largest (by volume): **Iguazú Falls, Brazil – Argentina –** 1,756 m^3 (62,012 ft^3) of water per second

Tallest buildings

Gran Torre
Santiago, Chile
300 m (984 ft)

Parque Central Complex, East Tower
Caracas, Venezuela
225 m (738 ft)

Parque Central Complex, West Tower
Caracas, Venezuela
225 m (738 ft)

Torre Colpatria
Bogotá, Colombia
196 m (643 ft)

Titanium La Portada
Santiago, Chile
194 m (636 ft)

Most visited cities (Visitors per year)

Lima, Peru
4.03 million

São Paulo, Brazil
2.3 million

Buenos Aires, Argentina
2.02 million

Rio de Janeiro, Brazil
1.37 million

Bogotá, Colombia
1.26 million

South America's extreme points

Northernmost point:
Punta Gallinas,
Colombia, 12° 28′ N

Easternmost point:
Ilhas Martin Vaz,
Brazil, 28° 51′ W

Westernmost point:
Galapagos Islands, Ecuador,
92° 00′ W

Southernmost point:
Cape Horn,
Chile, 55° 59′ S

Longest bridge

Rio Niterói Bridge,
Guanabara Bay,
Brazil – **13.29 km
(8.25 miles)**

Lowest point

Laguna del Carbón,
Santa Cruz, Argentina –
-104.9 m (-344 ft)

This is the seventh-lowest point
on Earth's surface.

Landlocked countries 2 – Bolivia and Paraguay

Highest mountains

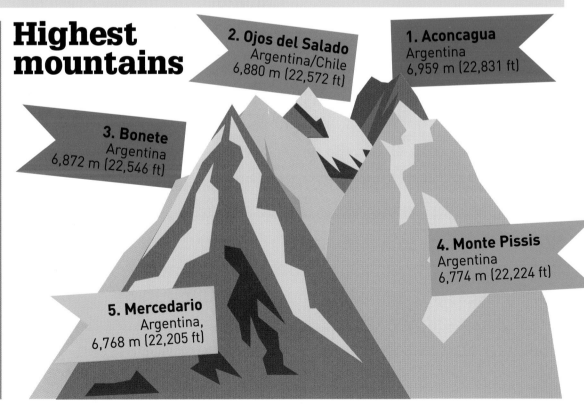

2. Ojos del Salado
Argentina/Chile
6,880 m (22,572 ft)

1. Aconcagua
Argentina
6,959 m (22,831 ft)

3. Bonete
Argentina
6,872 m (22,546 ft)

4. Monte Pissis
Argentina
6,774 m (22,224 ft)

5. Mercedario
Argentina,
6,768 m (22,205 ft)

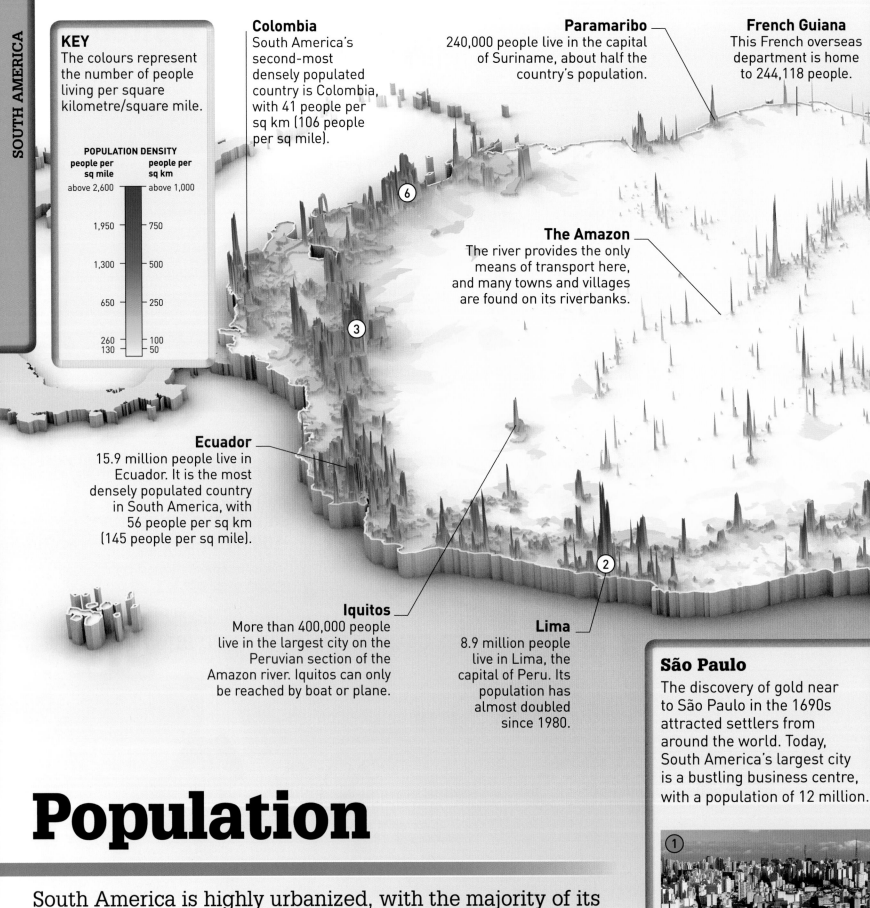

KEY
The colours represent the number of people living per square kilometre/square mile.

POPULATION DENSITY

people per sq mile	people per sq km
above 2,600	above 1,000
1,950	750
1,300	500
650	250
260	100
130	50

Colombia
South America's second-most densely populated country is Colombia, with 41 people per sq km (106 people per sq mile).

Paramaribo
240,000 people live in the capital of Suriname, about half the country's population.

French Guiana
This French overseas department is home to 244,118 people.

The Amazon
The river provides the only means of transport here, and many towns and villages are found on its riverbanks.

Ecuador
15.9 million people live in Ecuador. It is the most densely populated country in South America, with 56 people per sq km (145 people per sq mile).

Iquitos
More than 400,000 people live in the largest city on the Peruvian section of the Amazon river. Iquitos can only be reached by boat or plane.

Lima
8.9 million people live in Lima, the capital of Peru. Its population has almost doubled since 1980.

São Paulo
The discovery of gold near to São Paulo in the 1690s attracted settlers from around the world. Today, South America's largest city is a bustling business centre, with a population of 12 million.

Tower blocks and modern architecture dominate the centre of São Paulo.

Population

South America is highly urbanized, with the majority of its population living in cities such as Lima and Bogotá in the north west, or São Paulo and Rio de Janeiro on the east coast of Brazil. By contrast, Amazonia, the Altiplano plateau, and Patagonia remain sparsely populated.

Brasília
Brazil's capital was planned from scratch, and was only finished in 1960. Today, it is home to 2.9 million people.

South America's largest cities
The list below is based on the number of people living inside a city's boundaries.

1. **São Paulo, Brazil – 12 million**
2. **Lima, Peru – 8.9 million**
3. **Bogotá, Colombia – 7.9 million**
4. **Rio de Janeiro, Brazil – 6.5 million**
5. **Santiago, Chile – 5.5 million**
6. **Caracas, Venezuela – 3.3 million**
7. **Buenos Aires, Argentina – 3 million**
8. **Salvador, Brazil – 2.9 million**
9. **Brasília, Brazil – 2.9 million**
10. **Fortaleza, Brazil – 2.6 million**

Rio de Janeiro, Brazil's second-largest city, was the country's capital until 1960.

Santa Cruz
The largest city in Bolivia is Santa Cruz, with a population of 1.4 million. It is one of the fastest growing cities in South America – its population has increased by a third in the past 10 years.

Chile
Most people in Chile live in the central region, home to the country's three largest cities: Santiago, Valparaíso, and Concepción.

Falkland Islands
Fewer than 3,000 people live on these islands, many of them working as sheep farmers. It is the least densely populated territory in South America.

The Trans-Amazonian Highway
Running from João Pessoa in the east to the Amazonian city of Lábrea, the Trans-Amazonian Highway is about 4,000 km (2,485 miles) long.

Meeting of waters
The Rio Negro's dark water meets the muddy Amazon near Manaus in Brazil. Their waters do not immediately mix, creating a two-tone river.

Los Llanos
Rains flood this vast grassland once a year, turning it into a huge temporary marshland. It is home to many species of water birds, and the rare Orinoco crocodile.

Peruvian rainforest
The rainforest covers about 60 per cent of Peru. As well as lowland Amazonian jungle, there is highland rainforest, which is home to many unique species.

Belén
Buildings are attached to stilts in the Peruvian village of Belén. The houses float on the river itself, rising and falling with its waters.

Nevado Mismi
The source of the Amazon river lies at the foot of a cliff face on Nevado Mismi, a mountain in the Peruvian Andes. It is marked by a cross.

VENEZUELA

Llanos

Orinoco

Pakarai Moun

Guian

Cordillera Occidental

Cordillera Oriental

Meta

COLOMBIA

Guaviare

Apaporis

Uaupés

Río Negr

Serra do Traíra

Japurá

Caquetá

Putumayo

Napo

Amazon

A m

Marañón

Javari

Juruá

Ucayali

P E R U

Purus

A n d e s

PACIFIC OCEAN

Lima

Cordiller

Lak Titi

THE AMAZON BASIN RECEIVES AN AVERAGE 2.3 M (7.5 FT) OF

Kaieteur Falls
Waterfalls are rare in the Amazon Basin, but Kaieteur Falls, in Guyana, is 226 m (741 ft) high – four times higher than Niagara Falls.

GUYANA

ighlands

Acarai Mountains

Branco

Serra do Jatapu

A T L A N T I C
O C E A N

Planalto
Maracanaquará

Amazon

Ilha de Marajó
The largest river island in the world, Marajó is about the size of Switzerland.

Ilha de Marajó

Belém

Xingu

Tocantins

Iriri

The Amazon River
The Nile might be longer, but the Amazon carries more water than any other river on Earth – approximately 20 per cent of all the water that reaches the sea from the world's rivers.

azon

o   n

Manaus

Madeira

Purus

Tapajós

Serra do Cachimbo

São Manuel

Serra Formosa

Pororoca
The Amazon river's tidal bore, the Pororoca, is a large wave that occurs when there's a new or full moon. It can reach up to 8 m (26 ft) high, and is popular with surfers.

Lábrea
The Trans-Amazonian Highway ends its 4,000-km (2,500-mile) journey from João Pessoa to Lábrea here.

Porto Velho

Mamoré

Guaporé

Chapada dos Parecis

Planalto de
Mato Grosso

B
O
L
I
V
I
A

riental

La Paz

Altiplano

Cordillera
Occidental

Amazon Basin

Home to the world's largest rainforest, the Amazon Basin covers an area almost as large as Australia. It is Earth's most dynamic ecosystem; 3 million different types of plant and animal live in its lush jungle, and new species are still being discovered there every year.

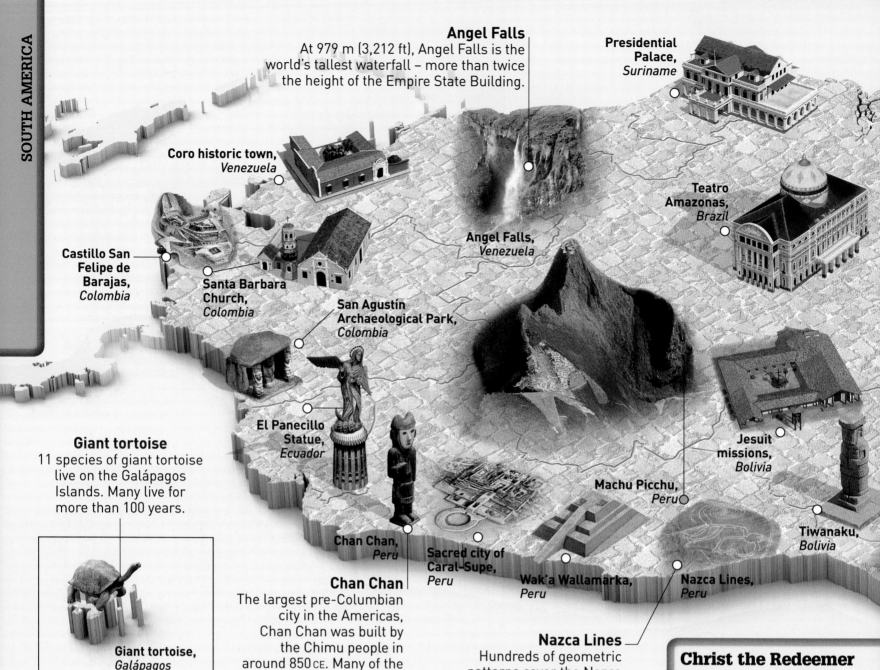

Angel Falls
At 979 m (3,212 ft), Angel Falls is the world's tallest waterfall – more than twice the height of the Empire State Building.

Presidential Palace, *Suriname*

Coro historic town, *Venezuela*

Angel Falls, *Venezuela*

Teatro Amazonas, *Brazil*

Castillo San Felipe de Barajas, *Colombia*

Santa Barbara Church, *Colombia*

San Agustín Archaeological Park, *Colombia*

El Panecillo Statue, *Ecuador*

Jesuit missions, *Bolivia*

Machu Picchu, *Peru*

Tiwanaku, *Bolivia*

Giant tortoise
11 species of giant tortoise live on the Galápagos Islands. Many live for more than 100 years.

Giant tortoise, *Galápagos*

Chan Chan, *Peru*

Sacred city of Caral-Supe, *Peru*

Wak'a Wallamarka, *Peru*

Nazca Lines, *Peru*

Chan Chan
The largest pre-Columbian city in the Americas, Chan Chan was built by the Chimu people in around 850 CE. Many of the city's walls have crumbled over time, but several statues have survived.

Nazca Lines
Hundreds of geometric patterns cover the Nazca Desert. About 70 of them are images of animals, but they can only be seen in full from an aircraft.

Christ the Redeemer
Looking down from the summit of Mount Corcovado onto Rio de Janeiro, Christ the Redeemer is one of the continent's best-loved landmarks. Finished in 1931, the 39-m (128-ft) tall statue took five years to build.

Famous landmarks

South America is home to an incredible wealth of cultural sites, ranging from the Inca ruins of Machu Picchu to the modern architecture of Brasília. It also boasts awe-inspiring natural wonders, such as Venezuela's Angel Falls and the glaciers of Chile and Argentina.

○ The giant statue of Jesus Christ towers over Brazil's second city, Rio de Janeiro.

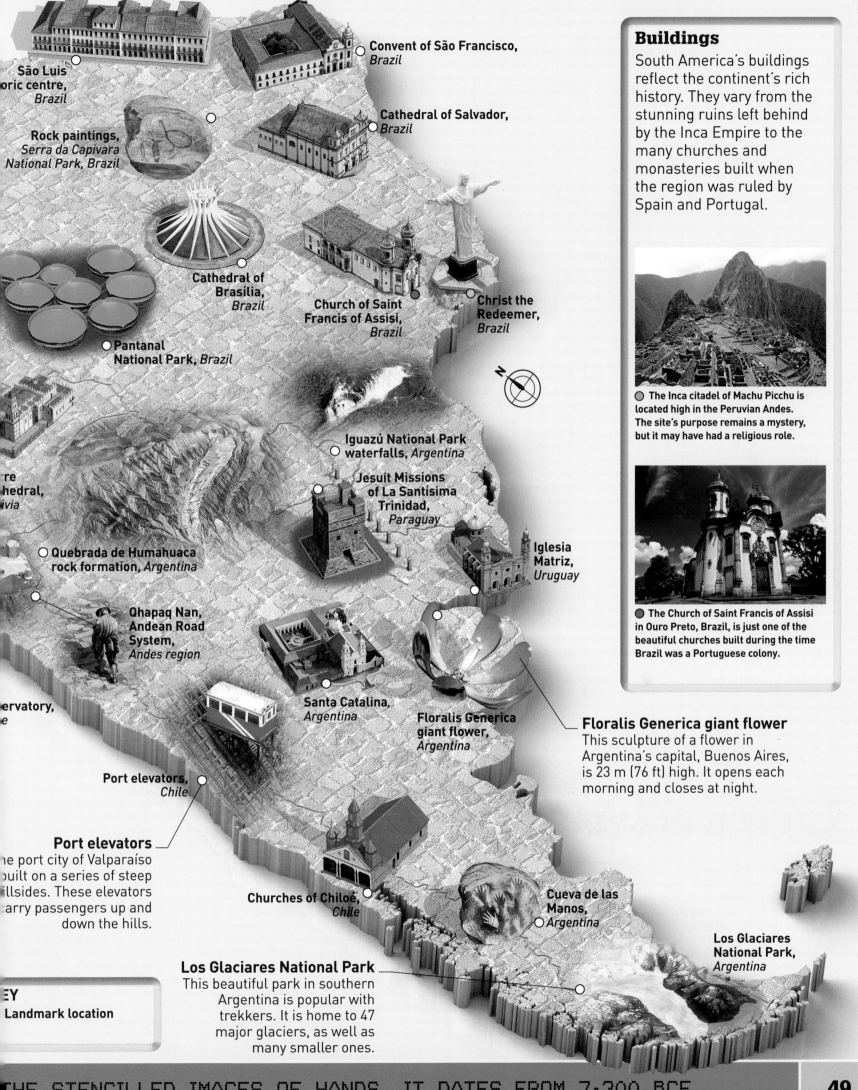

São Luis
Historic centre,
Brazil

Convent of São Francisco,
Brazil

Rock paintings,
*Serra da Capivara
National Park, Brazil*

Cathedral of Salvador,
Brazil

**Cathedral of
Brasília,**
Brazil

**Church of Saint
Francis of Assisi,**
Brazil

**Christ the
Redeemer,**
Brazil

**Pantanal
National Park,** *Brazil*

re
hedral,
ivia

**Iguazú National Park
waterfalls,** *Argentina*

**Jesuit Missions
of La Santísima
Trinidad,**
Paraguay

○ **Quebrada de Humahuaca
rock formation,** *Argentina*

**Iglesia
Matriz,**
Uruguay

○ **Qhapaq Nan,
Andean Road
System,**
Andes region

ervatory,
e

Santa Catalina,
Argentina

**Floralis Generica
giant flower,**
Argentina

Port elevators,
Chile

Port elevators
e port city of Valparaíso
built on a series of steep
illsides. These elevators
arry passengers up and
down the hills.

Churches of Chiloé,
Chile

**Cueva de las
Manos,**
Argentina

**Los Glaciares
National Park,**
Argentina

Los Glaciares National Park
This beautiful park in southern
Argentina is popular with
trekkers. It is home to 47
major glaciers, as well as
many smaller ones.

EY

□ **Landmark location**

Buildings
South America's buildings
reflect the continent's rich
history. They vary from the
stunning ruins left behind
by the Inca Empire to the
many churches and
monasteries built when
the region was ruled by
Spain and Portugal.

● The Inca citadel of Machu Picchu is
located high in the Peruvian Andes.
The site's purpose remains a mystery,
but it may have had a religious role.

● The Church of Saint Francis of Assisi
in Ouro Preto, Brazil, is just one of the
beautiful churches built during the time
Brazil was a Portuguese colony.

Floralis Generica giant flower
This sculpture of a flower in
Argentina's capital, Buenos Aires,
is 23 m (76 ft) high. It opens each
morning and closes at night.

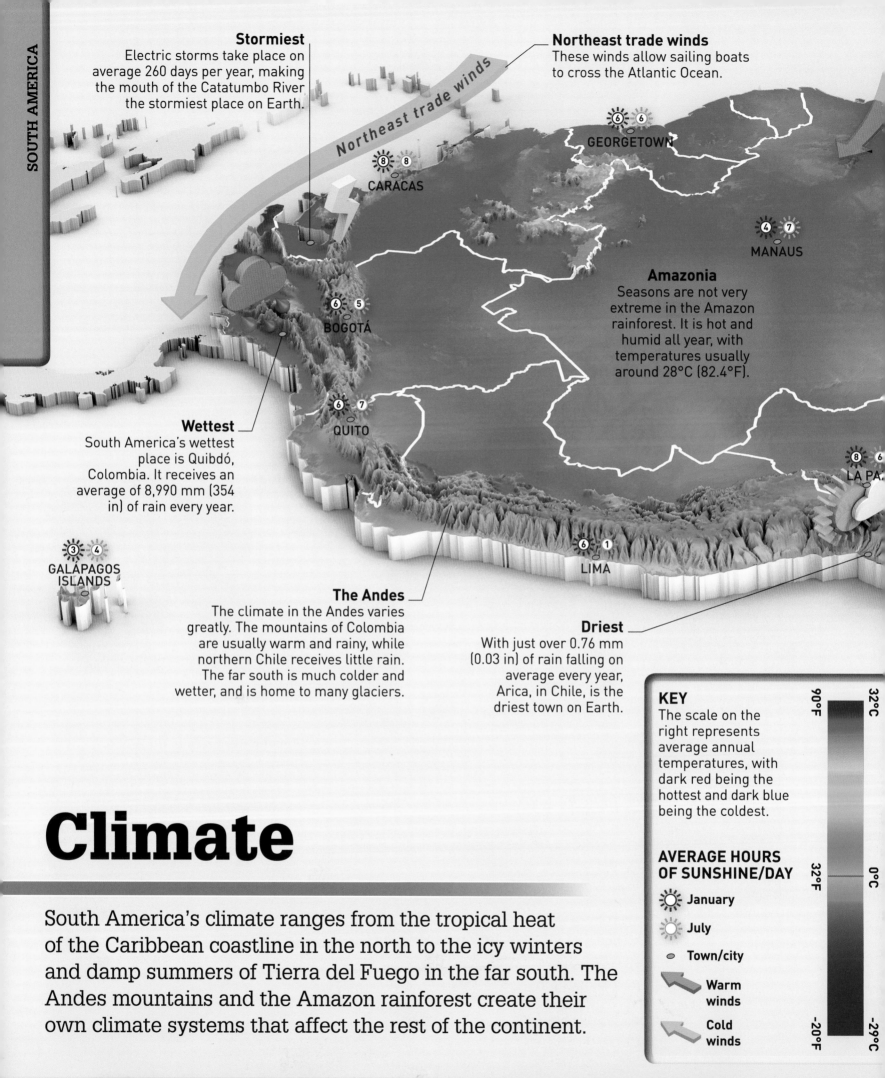

Stormiest
Electric storms take place on average 260 days per year, making the mouth of the Catatumbo River the stormiest place on Earth.

Northeast trade winds
These winds allow sailing boats to cross the Atlantic Ocean.

Northeast trade winds

GEORGETOWN
6 6

CARACAS
8 8

MANAUS
4 7

Amazonia
Seasons are not very extreme in the Amazon rainforest. It is hot and humid all year, with temperatures usually around 28°C (82.4°F).

BOGOTÁ
6 5

QUITO
6 7

LA PA...
8 6

Wettest
South America's wettest place is Quibdó, Colombia. It receives an average of 8,990 mm (354 in) of rain every year.

GALÁPAGOS ISLANDS
3 4

LIMA
6 1

The Andes
The climate in the Andes varies greatly. The mountains of Colombia are usually warm and rainy, while northern Chile receives little rain. The far south is much colder and wetter, and is home to many glaciers.

Driest
With just over 0.76 mm (0.03 in) of rain falling on average every year, Arica, in Chile, is the driest town on Earth.

KEY
The scale on the right represents average annual temperatures, with dark red being the hottest and dark blue being the coldest.

90°F 32°C
32°F 0°C
-20°F -29°C

AVERAGE HOURS OF SUNSHINE/DAY
- January
- July
- Town/city
- Warm winds
- Cold winds

Climate

South America's climate ranges from the tropical heat of the Caribbean coastline in the north to the icy winters and damp summers of Tierra del Fuego in the far south. The Andes mountains and the Amazon rainforest create their own climate systems that affect the rest of the continent.

THERE ARE WEATHER STATIONS IN THE ATACAMA DESERT THAT

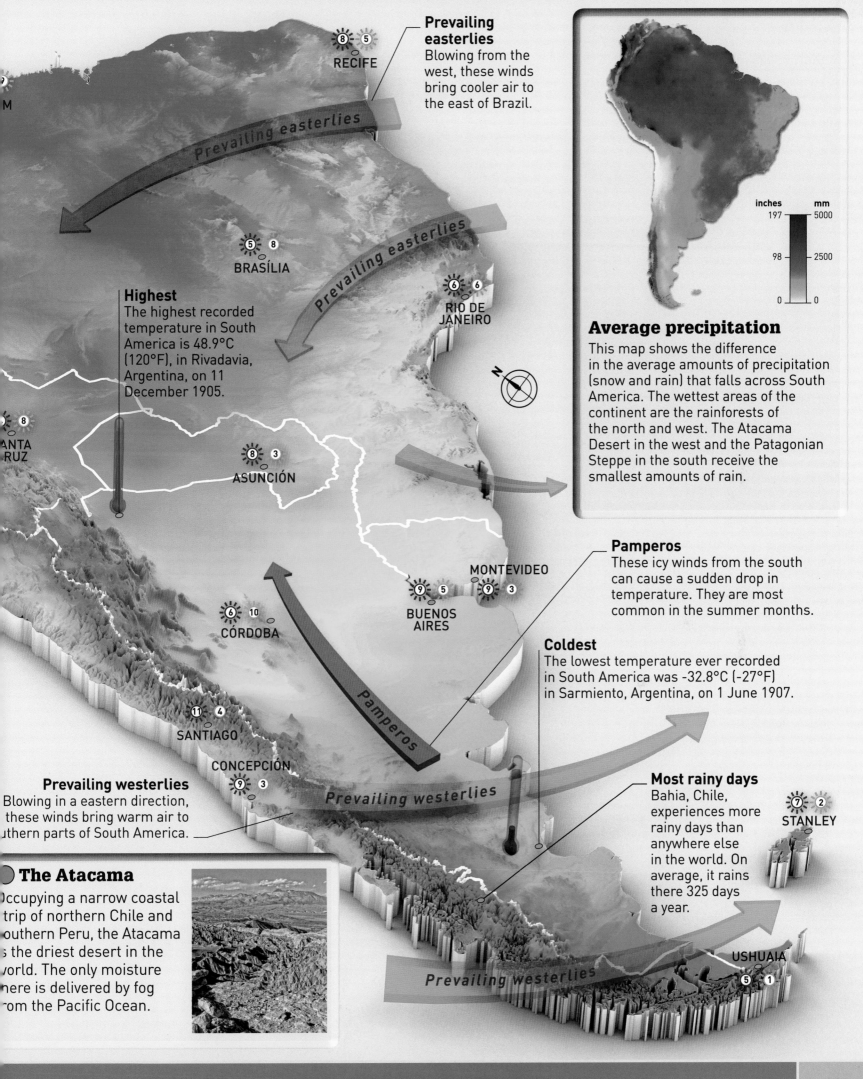

Prevailing easterlies
Blowing from the west, these winds bring cooler air to the east of Brazil.

8 5
RECIFE

Prevailing easterlies

Prevailing easterlies

5 8
BRASÍLIA

6 6
RIO DE JANEIRO

Highest
The highest recorded temperature in South America is 48.9°C (120°F), in Rivadavia, Argentina, on 11 December 1905.

8
ANTA RUZ

8 3
ASUNCIÓN

N

Average precipitation
This map shows the difference in the average amounts of precipitation (snow and rain) that falls across South America. The wettest areas of the continent are the rainforests of the north and west. The Atacama Desert in the west and the Patagonian Steppe in the south receive the smallest amounts of rain.

inches | mm
197 | 5000
98 | 2500
0 | 0

Pamperos
These icy winds from the south can cause a sudden drop in temperature. They are most common in the summer months.

9 5 **9 3**
MONTEVIDEO

6 10
CÓRDOBA

9
BUENOS AIRES

Coldest
The lowest temperature ever recorded in South America was -32.8°C (-27°F) in Sarmiento, Argentina, on 1 June 1907.

Pamperos

11 4
SANTIAGO

9 3
CONCEPCIÓN

Prevailing westerlies
Blowing in a eastern direction, these winds bring warm air to uthern parts of South America.

Prevailing westerlies

Most rainy days
Bahia, Chile, experiences more rainy days than anywhere else in the world. On average, it rains there 325 days a year.

7 2
STANLEY

The Atacama
Occupying a narrow coastal trip of northern Chile and outhern Peru, the Atacama s the driest desert in the world. The only moisture here is delivered by fog rom the Pacific Ocean.

USHUAIA

Prevailing westerlies

5 1

Common vampire bat
This bat drinks the blood of tapirs and cattle.

Goliath bird-eating spider
Despite its name, the world's largest spider prefers eating small rodents or toads.

Bull shark
This formidable hunter thrives in both freshwater and saltwater.

Hoatzin
Also known as the stinkbird. Its chick have "wing claws" for clambering through branches.

Capuchin monkey
Intelligent and sociable, this monkey forages for food in the treetops.

Jaguar
The rainforest' largest killer is lone, nocturna hunter.

Bald uakari
This monkey's bright red face is seen as highly attractive in a mate.

Spectacled caiman
A good swimmer, it hunts fish such as piranhas.

Harpy eagle
This large raptor can snatch sloths and monkeys from trees.

Tiger shark
Coastal waters and estuaries are home to this dangerous shark.

Spectacled bear
The continent's only bear lives in mountain forests and eats fruit and nuts.

Ocelot
A nocturnal hunter, this small cat preys on rodents. It is also an excellent swimmer.

Puma
Found throughout the Americas, the puma thrives in deserts, prairies, and forests.

Great white shark
This dangerous predator can live for up to 70 years

Darwin's finches
This group of small birds helped Charles Darwin to develop his theory of evolution.

Wildlife

The grasslands, mountains, and rainforests of South America contain an incredible variety of plant and animal species. This vast range of habitats is home to many species of birds, mammals, and amphibians that are found nowhere else on Earth.

BIOMES
Tropical broadleaf forest is widespread in the north, before it gives way to temperate grasslands and temperate broadleaf forest in the south.

- Ice
- Temperate broadleaf forest
- Temperate grassland
- Mediterranean
- Tropical broadleaf forest
- Tropical dry broadleaf forest
- Mountain
- Desert
- Flooded grassland
- Mangrove

THE JAGUAR IS AN EXCELLENT SWIMMER AND HAS EVEN

Amazonian river dolphin
Its long snout is used to explore the river bed and get between tree roots.

Toucan
This bird rests its beak on its back while sleeping.

Capybara
Riverbanks and wetland areas are home to this giant rodent.

Amazonian wildlife
The Amazon rainforest is home to an incredible range of wildlife. Around 130 species of monkey, 400 species of frog, 500 species of reptile, and at least 1,500 different species of bird live in the world's largest rainforest.

The brightly coloured macaw is the largest of all the parrots. It eats a varied diet of fruit, nuts, and seeds.

Poison-dart frog
Has a brightly coloured skin to warn predators that it is poisonous.

Peccary
These pig-like creatures form groups to fend off enemies.

Red-bellied piranha
A shoal of these fish can strip its prey to bare bones in minutes.

Golden lion tamarin
This elegant monkey has a beautiful mane and lives in large family groups.

Humpback whale
These ocean giants sing in order to attract a mate.

Guanaco
The wild ancestor of the llama is adapted to high-altitude life.

Giant anteater
Huge front claws and a long snout help the anteater to raid termite nests.

Armadillo
The only mammal to have body armour, the armadillo rolls itself into a ball when threatened.

Yellow anaconda
Rarely seen out of water, this snake can grow up to 4.4 m (14.4 ft) in length.

Geoffroy's cat
This tiny feline is an excellent climber and preys on birds.

Darwin's rhea
When threatened, this flightless bird flees in a zigzag pattern.

Andean condor
With a wingspan of more than 3 m (10 ft), this bird can glide for vast distances.

Southern sea lion
Squid and octopus form much of this agile hunter's diet.

Patagonian mara
This rodent rears its young in communal burrows on the grassland.

Southern right whale
Following years of exploitation by whalers, numbers are steadily increasing.

Magellanic penguin
Only 65 cm (26 in) tall, this penguin hunts small fish.

Caracas
89 per cent of Venezuela's population live in towns or cities, with 5.3 million people living in the country's capital, Caracas.

Guyana
Less than 30 per cent of Guyana's population of 735,900 live in towns or cities

Ecuador
Many people in Ecuador live in the Andean highland region known as La Sierra. Important cities here include Cuenca and the capital, Quito.

Guayaquil
More than 5 million people live in and around Ecuador's most populous city. It is an important port and business centre.

Lima
Nearly 10 million people live in the area in and around the Peruvian capital.

Almost **one half** of South America's population lives **in Brazil**.

By night

The brightly lit urban areas of Ecuador, Colombia, and Venezuela dominate the northwest of the continent. The cities of southeast Brazil, meanwhile, contrast sharply with the dark expanses of Amazonia, in which only occasional dots of light mark the rainforest's few settlements.

● **Manaus**
Located at the heart of the Amazon rainforest, Manaus, with a population of 2 million, is the largest city in Amazonia. This lively port made its wealth in the 19th century through the rubber trade.

The opera house in Manaus is one of the grandest buildings in Amazonia.

Salvador
The largest city in the north east of Brazil, Salvador has a population of 2.9 million.

Brazil
More than 80 million people live in the urban areas that dominate Brazil's south east.

Porto Alegre
1.5 million people live in Brazil's 10th-largest city.

● Buenos Aires
Three million people live in the Argentinian capital. As well as being an important political and business centre, Buenos Aires is known for its lively nightlife, and has a superb choice of theatres, restaurants, and music venues.

The Argentinian tango remains popular in the bars and cafés of Buenos Aires.

Uruguay
95.3 per cent of Uruguay's population of 3.4 million live in towns or cities – the highest percentage of any South American country.

Comodoro Rivadavia
182,631 people live in Comodoro-Rivadavia – the most southerly city in South America with a population of more than 150,000.

Santiago
One third of Chile's population of 17.5 million live in the country's capital city.

KEY
Illuminated areas on the map reflect urban, built-up areas and roads, in contrast to rural regions.

■ **Rural area**

▨ **Urban area**

Patagonia
Fewer than 2 million people live in the southernmost part of the continent.

AFRICA

Africa from space
The Equator splits Africa between the northern and southern hemispheres. It is bordered by the Mediterranean, the Red Sea, and the Atlantic and Indian Oceans.

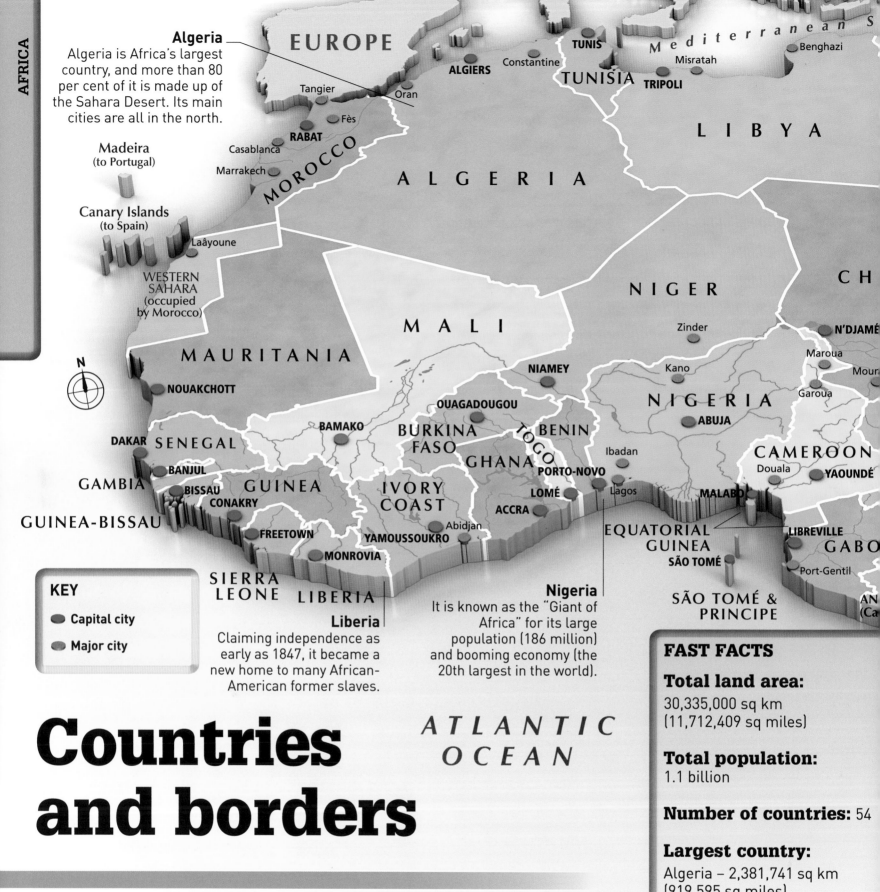

Algeria
Algeria is Africa's largest country, and more than 80 per cent of it is made up of the Sahara Desert. Its main cities are all in the north.

EUROPE

M e d i t e r r a n e a n S

TUNIS
Benghazi
Misratah
Constantine
ALGIERS
TUNISIA
Tangier
TRIPOLI
Oran
Fès
RABAT
Casablanca
Marrakech
MOROCCO

Madeira
(to Portugal)

L I B Y A

A L G E R I A

Canary Islands
(to Spain)
Laâyoune

WESTERN
SAHARA
(occupied
by Morocco)

N I G E R

C H

N'DJAMÉ

M A L I

Zinder
Maroua
Mour

MAURITANIA

Kano
Garoua

N
NOUAKCHOTT
NIAMEY
N I G E R I A

OUAGADOUGOU
ABUJA

BAMAKO
BURKINA
FASO
BENIN
CAMEROON

DAKAR SENEGAL
GHANA
TOGO
Ibadan
Douala YAOUNDÉ

BANJUL
PORTO-NOVO
Lagos
GAMBIA
IVORY
COAST
LOMÉ
BISSAU
GUINEA
MALABO
LIBREVILLE
CONAKRY
ACCRA
EQUATORIAL
GUINEA
GABO
GUINEA-BISSAU
Abidjan
SÃO TOMÉ
FREETOWN
YAMOUSSOUKRO
Port-Gentil
MONROVIA
AN
(Ca

SIERRA
LEONE LIBERIA

Nigeria
It is known as the "Giant of Africa" for its large population (186 million) and booming economy (the 20th largest in the world).

SÃO TOMÉ &
PRINCIPE

Liberia
Claiming independence as early as 1847, it became a new home to many African-American former slaves.

KEY
● Capital city
● Major city

*ATLANTIC
OCEAN*

Countries and borders

FAST FACTS

Total land area:
30,335,000 sq km
(11,712,409 sq miles)

Total population:
1.1 billion

Number of countries: 54

Largest country:
Algeria – 2,381,741 sq km
(919,595 sq miles)

Smallest country:
Seychelles –
455 sq km (176 sq miles)

**Largest country
population:**
Nigeria – 186 million

Africa's different kingdoms were brutally split up between European nations in the 19th century. After World War Two, struggle for independence, as well as civil wars, created new nations, re-drawn borders, and disputed territories.

ETHIOPIA IS THE ONLY COUNTRY IN AFRICA THAT HAS

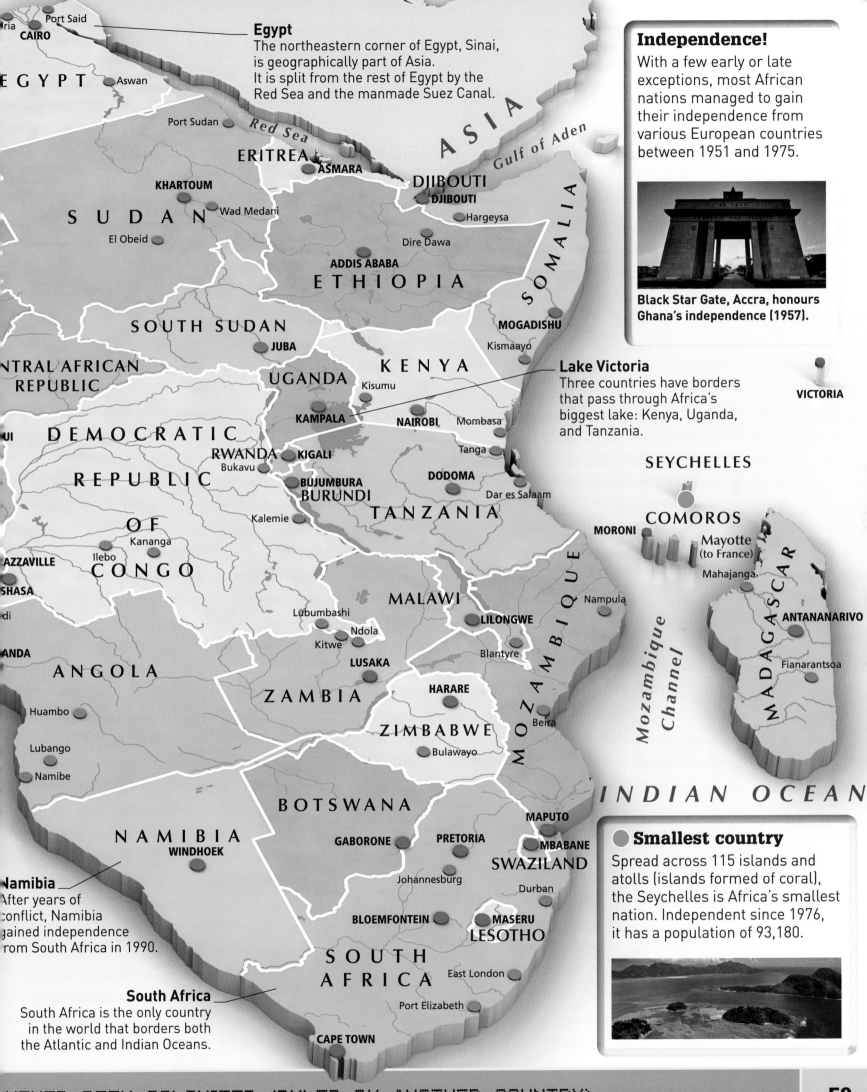

Port Said
CAIRO
ria
EGYPT
Aswan

Egypt
The northeastern corner of Egypt, Sinai, is geographically part of Asia. It is split from the rest of Egypt by the Red Sea and the manmade Suez Canal.

ASIA

Port Sudan
Red Sea
Gulf of Aden

ERITREA
ASMARA

DJIBOUTI
DJIBOUTI
Hargeysa

KHARTOUM
SUDAN
Wad Medani

El Obeid

Dire Dawa

ADDIS ABABA
ETHIOPIA

SOMALIA

SOUTH SUDAN

MOGADISHU
Kismaayo

JUBA
KENYA

NTRAL AFRICAN REPUBLIC
UGANDA
Kisumu
KAMPALA
NAIROBI
Mombasa

ui
DEMOCRATIC

RWANDA
KIGALI
Bukavu
BUJUMBURA
BURUNDI
Kalemie
Tanga

REPUBLIC
DODOMA
Dar es Salaam

OF
Kananga
TANZANIA

AZZAVILLE
Ilebo
CONGO

SHASA
di

MALAWI

Lubumbashi
Ndola
Kitwe
LILONGWE
Blantyre

ANDA
LUSAKA

ANGOLA
Nampula

Huambo
ZAMBIA
HARARE

Lubango
ZIMBABWE
Beira

Namibe
Bulawayo

BOTSWANA

NAMIBIA
WINDHOEK
MAPUTO

GABORONE
PRETORIA
MBABANE
SWAZILAND
Johannesburg
Durban

BLOEMFONTEIN
MASERU
LESOTHO

SOUTH
AFRICA
East London

Port Elizabeth

CAPE TOWN

Lake Victoria
Three countries have borders that pass through Africa's biggest lake: Kenya, Uganda, and Tanzania.

VICTORIA

SEYCHELLES

COMOROS
MORONI
Mayotte
(to France)
Mahajanga

MADAGASCAR
ANTANANARIVO

Fianarantsoa

Mozambique Channel

MOZAMBIQUE

INDIAN OCEAN

Namibia
After years of conflict, Namibia gained independence from South Africa in 1990.

South Africa
South Africa is the only country in the world that borders both the Atlantic and Indian Oceans.

Independence!
With a few early or late exceptions, most African nations managed to gain their independence from various European countries between 1951 and 1975.

Black Star Gate, Accra, honours Ghana's independence (1957).

● **Smallest country**
Spread across 115 islands and atolls (islands formed of coral), the Seychelles is Africa's smallest nation. Independent since 1976, it has a population of 93,180.

KEY
The colours on the map represent the height of the land in relation to sea level.

ELEVATION

Feet	Metres
above 26,247	above 8,000
22,965	7,000
19,685	6,000
16,404	5,000
13,123	4,000
9,842	3,000
6,560	2,000
3,280	1,000
Sea level 0	0 Sea level

EUROPE

Mediterranean Sea

Gulf of Sirte

Qatt Depres

Great Sand Sea

We De

Lib

Atlas Mountains

Chott el Jerid

Grand Erg Occidental

Grand Erg Oriental

Erg Iguidi

Ahaggar

Tibesti

Erg Chech

Tanezrouft

Massif de l'Aïr

Ténéré

r

Taoudeni Basin

S

a

h

a

Lake Chad

Azaouad

S

a

h

e

l

Shebshi Mountains

N

Senegal

Niger

White Volta

Niger

Benue

Adamawa Highlands

Lake Volta

Cameroon Mountain
4,040 m / 13,250 ft

Niger Delta

Bight of Benin

Principe

Gulf of Guinea

São Tomé

River Niger
From its source in the Guinea Highlands, the Niger flows north, into the desert, and then back south, before flowing into the Gulf of Guinea.

Low-lying coasts
Mangroves, swamps, and sandy beaches line much of West Africa's coast.

Sahel
The dry grasslands of the Sahel are slowly turning into desert due to drought and human activity.

ATLANTIC OCEAN

Landscape

Africa has many extreme landscapes. Deserts spread across the north and south, while rainforests dominate the continent's tropical central and western parts. The land rises towards the east, culminating in the Ethiopian Highlands and the Great Rift Valley region, home to Africa's largest lakes and mountains.

FAST FACTS

① **Highest point:**
Kilimanjaro – 5,895 m (19,341 ft)

② **Longest river:**
Nile – 6,695 km (4,160 miles)

③ **Largest lake:**
Lake Victoria – 69,484 sq km (26,828 sq miles)

④ **Largest island:**
Madagascar – 594,000 sq km (229,345 sq miles)

THE CONGO BASIN, DRAINED BY THE CONGO RIVER, CONTAINS THE

A S I A

Delta

Nile

Eastern Desert

Lake Nasser

Nubian Desert

Nile ②

Red Sea

Blue Nile

White Nile

Ethiopian Highlands
This high plateau contains peaks of over 4,500 m (14,764 ft) and is home to Lake Tana, source of the Blue Nile.

Lake Tana

Ethiopian Highlands

Gulf of Aden

Horn of Africa

Ogaden

Shebeli

⬤ Sahara Desert

The world's largest hot desert, the Sahara spreads over 9,200,000 sq km (3,600,000 sq miles). It features huge dunes, arid gravel plains, craggy mountains, and old volcanoes, as well as a few oases.

Massif des Bongo

angi

Sudd

Uele

Lake Albert

Congo

Lake Victoria ③

Lake Turkana

Great Rift Valley

Juba

Kilimanjaro 5,895 m / 19,341 ft ①

Kilimanjaro
Africa's highest mountain is a long-extinct volcano. Its famous ice and snow cap is getting smaller every year.

Seychelles

Pemba

Zanzibar

C o n g o B a s i n

Great Rift Valley

Lake Tanganyika

Mitumba Range

Comoro Islands

uango

Kwilu

Kasai

Lake Nyasa

④ *Madagascar*

Bié Plateau

Muchinga Escarpment

Zambezi

Victoria Falls

Cunene

Okavango Delta
Seasonal flooding fills this large inland delta. Water drains into the Kalahari Desert, not the sea.

Okavango Delta

Ntwetwe Pan

Lundi

Limpopo

② River Nile

At 6,695 km (4,160 miles), the Nile is the world's longest river. It has two main tributaries, the Blue and White Niles, which join in Khartoum, Sudan, before the river flows through Egypt.

Kalahari Basin

Namib Desert

Kalahari Desert

Drakensberg

Orange River

Namib Desert
The extremely dry Namib Desert includes the Namib Sand Sea – giant astal dunes up to 300 m (985 ft) high, that are often swept in dense fogs.

Great Karoo

Cape of Good Hope

Fascinating facts

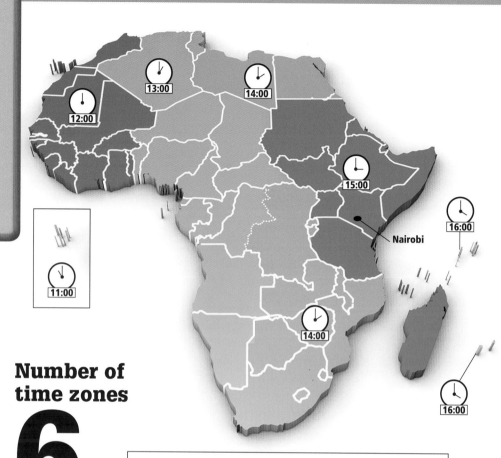

Nairobi

Number of time zones

6

The world is split into 39 time zones. Most are set whole hours ahead or behind Coordinated Universal Time (UCT) – the time at the Greenwich Meridian in London, UK. Some, however, are whole hours plus 30 or 45 minutes ahead or behind UCT. Therefore, on this map, if it was 12:00 in London, it would be 15:00 in Nairobi, Kenya (3 hours ahead of UCT).

COUNTRIES WITH THE MOST
NEIGHBOURS

Tanzania (8)
Burundi, **Democratic Republic of Congo**, Kenya, **Malawi**, Mozambique, **Rwanda**, Uganda, **Zambia**

Zambia (8)
Angola, **Botswana,** Democratic Republic of Congo, **Malawi**, Mozambique, **Namibia**, Tanzania, **Zimbabwe**

LONGEST BRIDGE
6th October Bridge, Cairo, Egypt – 20.5 km (12.7 miles)

16 LANDLOCKED COUNTRIES
Botswana ▪ **Burkina Faso** ▪ Burundi ▪ **Central African Republic** ▪ Chad ▪ **Ethiopia** ▪ Lesotho ▪ **Malawi** ▪ Mali ▪ **Niger** ▪ Rwanda ▪ **South Sudan** ▪ Swaziland ▪ **Uganda** ▪ Zambia ▪ **Zimbabwe**

Highest bridge
Bloukrans Bridge, Nature's Valley, Western Cape, South Africa – 216 m (709 ft)

Number of languages spoken more than
2,000

LAKES

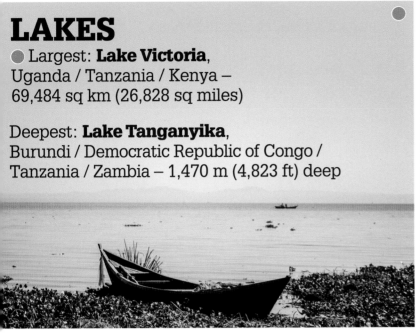

- Largest: **Lake Victoria**, Uganda / Tanzania / Kenya – 69,484 sq km (26,828 sq miles)

- Deepest: **Lake Tanganyika**, Burundi / Democratic Republic of Congo / Tanzania / Zambia – 1,470 m (4,823 ft) deep

WATERFALLS

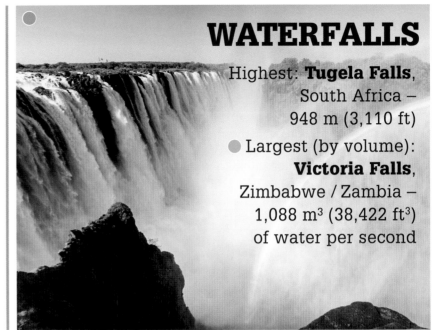

Highest: **Tugela Falls**, South Africa – 948 m (3,110 ft)

- Largest (by volume): **Victoria Falls**, Zimbabwe / Zambia – 1,088 m³ (38,422 ft³) of water per second

LONGEST COASTLINE Madagascar – 4,828 km (3,000 miles)

Busiest airport O.R. Tambo International, Johannesburg, South Africa – **19.164 million passengers per year**

Longest railway line
The Blue Train, Pretoria–Cape Town, South Africa – 1,600 km (994 miles)

Longest metro system
Cairo Metro, Egypt – 78 km (48 miles)

AFRICA'S EXTREME POINTS

Northernmost point:
Jalta, Tunisia
37° 31′ N

Easternmost point:
Raas Xaafuun, Somalia
51° 24′ E

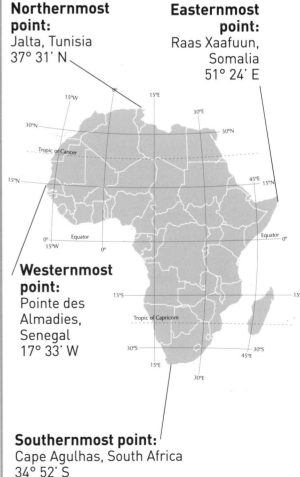

Westernmost point:
Pointe des Almadies, Senegal
17° 33′ W

Southernmost point:
Cape Agulhas, South Africa
34° 52′ S

Most visited cities

Johannesburg, S. Africa
3.6 million

Cairo, Egypt
1.5 million

Cape Town, S. Africa
1.4 million

Casablanca, Morocco
1.1 million

Durban, S. Africa
0.8 million

Most active volcano
Nyamuragira, **Democratic Republic of Congo**

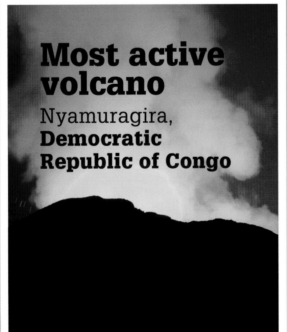

LOWEST POINT
Lake 'Assal, Djibouti – 156 m (512 ft) below sea level

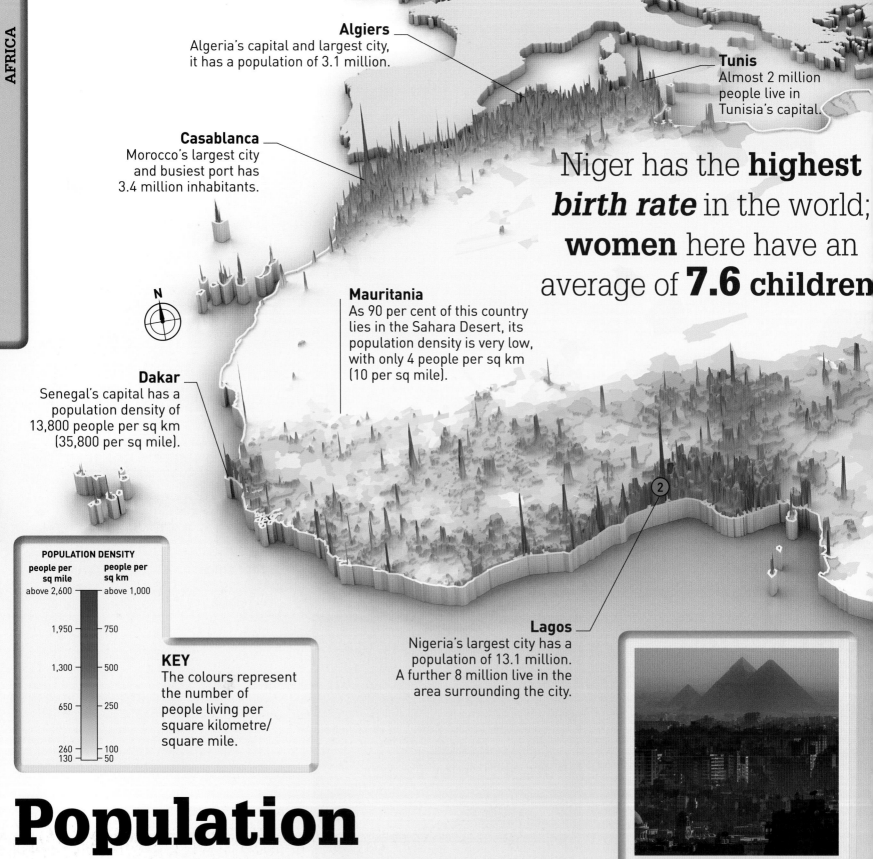

Algiers
Algeria's capital and largest city, it has a population of 3.1 million.

Tunis
Almost 2 million people live in Tunisia's capital.

Casablanca
Morocco's largest city and busiest port has 3.4 million inhabitants.

Niger has the **highest birth rate** in the world; **women** here have an average of **7.6 children**

Mauritania
As 90 per cent of this country lies in the Sahara Desert, its population density is very low, with only 4 people per sq km (10 per sq mile).

Dakar
Senegal's capital has a population density of 13,800 people per sq km (35,800 per sq mile).

POPULATION DENSITY

people per sq mile	people per sq km
above 2,600	above 1,000
1,950	750
1,300	500
650	250
260	100
130	50

KEY
The colours represent the number of people living per square kilometre/square mile.

Lagos
Nigeria's largest city has a population of 13.1 million. A further 8 million live in the area surrounding the city.

Population

Africa, the birthplace of our earliest human ancestors, is the second-most populous continent in the world (after Asia). But because the continent is so large, its average population density is low – only half that of Europe. In reality, some regions are very crowded, while others, like the Sahara, are almost deserted.

① Cairo, Egypt
Founded in ancient times and Egypt's capital since 1168, Cairo is Africa's largest city, with 18.7 million inhabitants. Greater Cairo sprawls in all directions, and includes the famous pyramids at Giza.

THE WORLD'S FIRST HOMININS (EARLY HUMANS) APPEARED IN

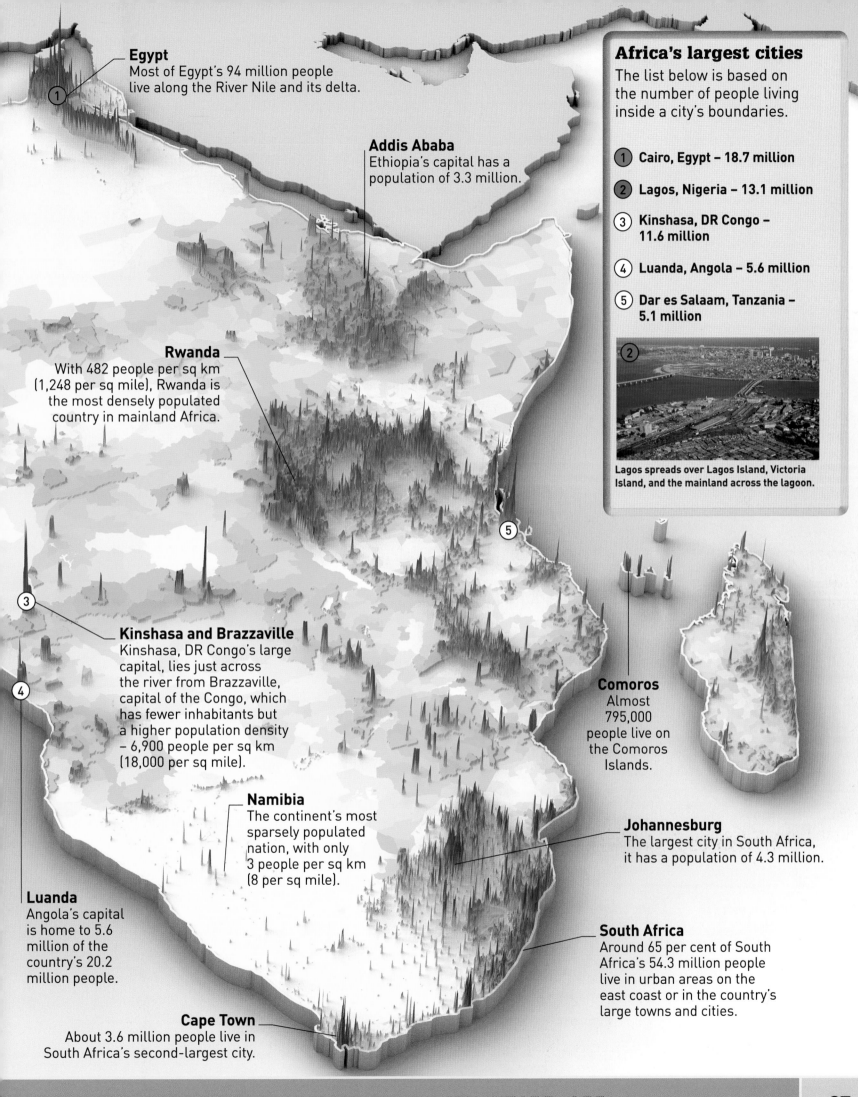

Egypt
Most of Egypt's 94 million people live along the River Nile and its delta.
①

Addis Ababa
Ethiopia's capital has a population of 3.3 million.

Rwanda
With 482 people per sq km (1,248 per sq mile), Rwanda is the most densely populated country in mainland Africa.

Kinshasa and Brazzaville
③
Kinshasa, DR Congo's large capital, lies just across the river from Brazzaville, capital of the Congo, which has fewer inhabitants but a higher population density – 6,900 people per sq km (18,000 per sq mile).

④

Namibia
The continent's most sparsely populated nation, with only 3 people per sq km (8 per sq mile).

Luanda
Angola's capital is home to 5.6 million of the country's 20.2 million people.

Cape Town
About 3.6 million people live in South Africa's second-largest city.

⑤

Comoros
Almost 795,000 people live on the Comoros Islands.

Johannesburg
The largest city in South Africa, it has a population of 4.3 million.

South Africa
Around 65 per cent of South Africa's 54.3 million people live in urban areas on the east coast or in the country's large towns and cities.

Africa's largest cities
The list below is based on the number of people living inside a city's boundaries.

① **Cairo, Egypt** – 18.7 million

② **Lagos, Nigeria** – 13.1 million

③ **Kinshasa, DR Congo** – 11.6 million

④ **Luanda, Angola** – 5.6 million

⑤ **Dar es Salaam, Tanzania** – 5.1 million

②
Lagos spreads over Lagos Island, Victoria Island, and the mainland across the lagoon.

Rwenzori Mountains
The snow-capped peaks of this range in the Western Rift Valley include Mount Stanley, Africa's third highest mountain at 5,109 m (16,762 ft).

Red Sea
Formed when the African and Arabian plates split apart, and still widening, this salty sea can reach over 30°C (86°F). Its coral reefs are teeming with fish.

Ethiopian Highlands

Ahmar Mountains

ETHIOPIA

Mēga Escarpr

SOUTH SUDAN

Lake Turkana

Cherangany Hills

Victoria Nile

Lake Kyoga

UGANDA

Lake Albert

Sese Islands

Lake Victoria

Ukerewe Island

Rubondo Island

Lake Victoria
Africa's largest lake lies on the plateau located between the Great Rift Valley's eastern and western branch. At its widest, it measures 337 km (209 miles) across.

Lake Edward

RWANDA

Lake Kivu

Western Rift Valley
The western branch of the Great Rift Valley is characterized by deep lakes and high mountain ranges.

BURUNDI

G r e a t   R i f

V a l l e y

Lake Tanganyika
The longest of the Rift Valley's many lakes, Tanganyika is, at 1,436 m (4,710 ft) deep, also the world's second deepest (after Lake Baikal).

Lake Tanganyika

IN THE FUTURE, THE LAND EAST OF THE RIFT WILL FORM A NEW

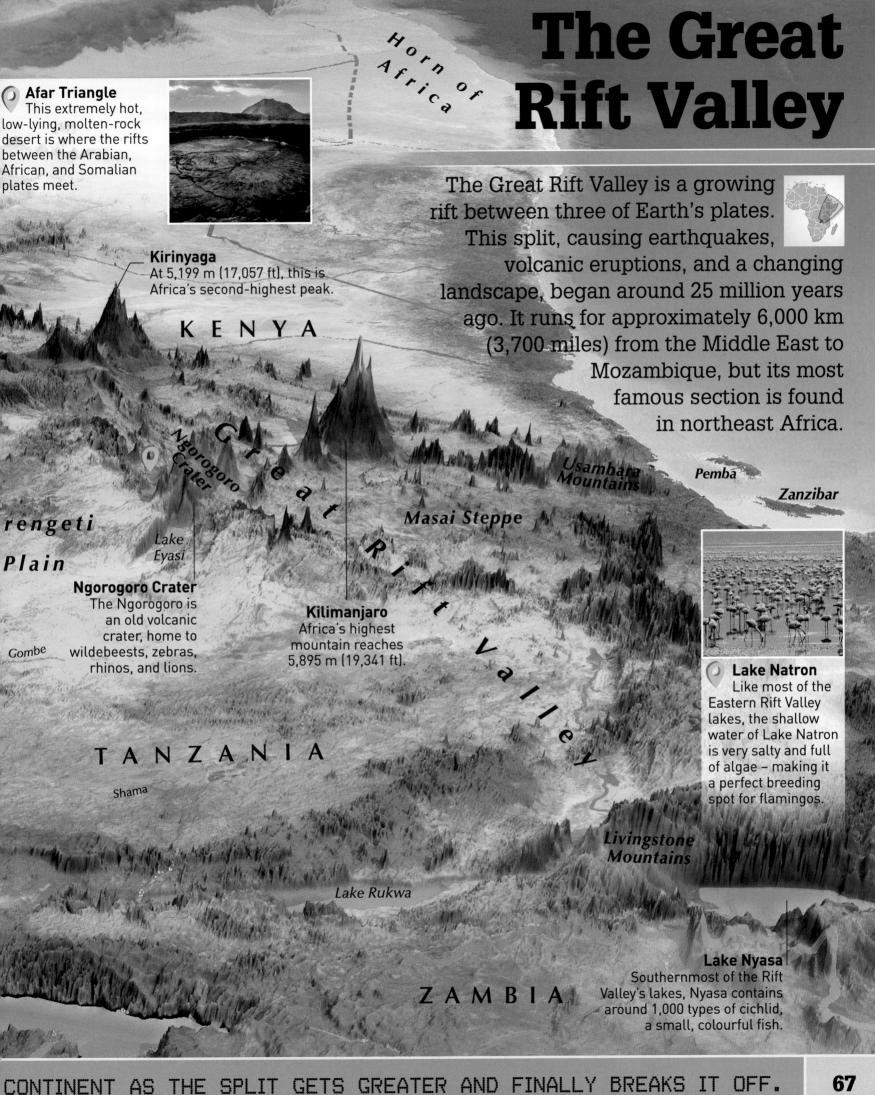

The Great Rift Valley

The Great Rift Valley is a growing rift between three of Earth's plates. This split, causing earthquakes, volcanic eruptions, and a changing landscape, began around 25 million years ago. It runs for approximately 6,000 km (3,700 miles) from the Middle East to Mozambique, but its most famous section is found in northeast Africa.

Afar Triangle
This extremely hot, low-lying, molten-rock desert is where the rifts between the Arabian, African, and Somalian plates meet.

Kirinyaga
At 5,199 m (17,057 ft), this is Africa's second-highest peak.

KENYA

Ngorogoro Crater

Great Rift Valley

rengeti

Plain

Lake Eyasi

Ngorogoro Crater
The Ngorogoro is an old volcanic crater, home to wildebeests, zebras, rhinos, and lions.

Gombe

Kilimanjaro
Africa's highest mountain reaches 5,895 m (19,341 ft).

Masai Steppe

Usambara Mountains

Pemba

Zanzibar

Lake Natron
Like most of the Eastern Rift Valley lakes, the shallow water of Lake Natron is very salty and full of algae – making it a perfect breeding spot for flamingos.

TANZANIA

Shama

Livingstone Mountains

Lake Rukwa

Lake Nyasa
Southernmost of the Rift Valley's lakes, Nyasa contains around 1,000 types of cichlid, a small, colourful fish.

ZAMBIA

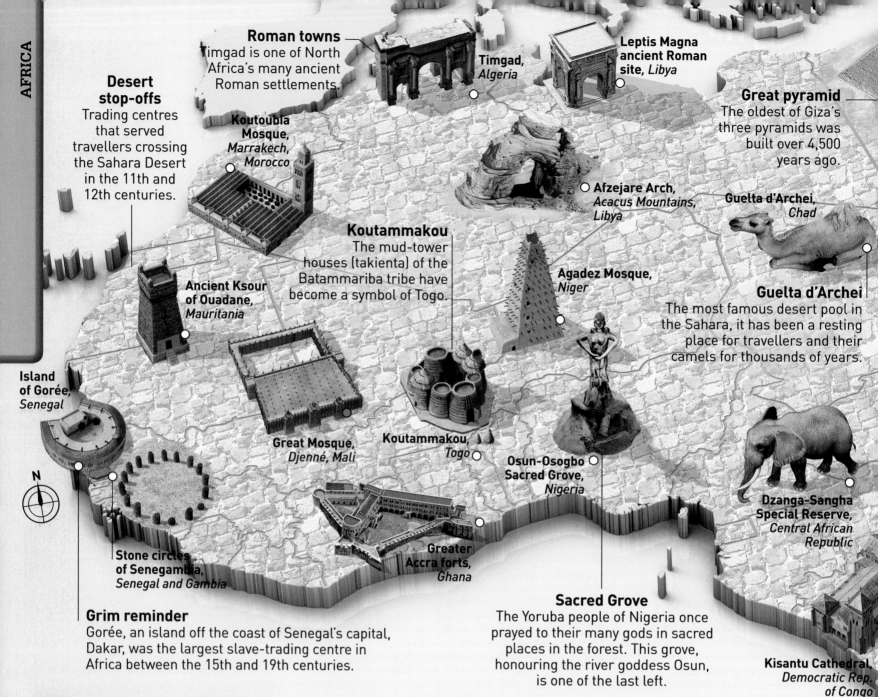

Roman towns
Timgad is one of North Africa's many ancient Roman settlements.

Timgad, *Algeria*

Leptis Magna ancient Roman site, *Libya*

Desert stop-offs
Trading centres that served travellers crossing the Sahara Desert in the 11th and 12th centuries.

Koutoubia Mosque, *Marrakech, Morocco*

Great pyramid
The oldest of Giza's three pyramids was built over 4,500 years ago.

Afzejare Arch, *Acacus Mountains, Libya*

Guelta d'Archei, *Chad*

Koutammakou
The mud-tower houses (takienta) of the Batammariba tribe have become a symbol of Togo.

Agadez Mosque, *Niger*

Ancient Ksour of Ouadane, *Mauritania*

Guelta d'Archei
The most famous desert pool in the Sahara, it has been a resting place for travellers and their camels for thousands of years.

Island of Gorée, *Senegal*

Great Mosque, *Djenné, Mali*

Koutammakou, *Togo*

Osun-Osogbo Sacred Grove, *Nigeria*

Stone circles of Senegambia, *Senegal and Gambia*

Greater Accra forts, *Ghana*

Dzanga-Sangha Special Reserve, *Central African Republic*

Grim reminder
Gorée, an island off the coast of Senegal's capital, Dakar, was the largest slave-trading centre in Africa between the 15th and 19th centuries.

Sacred Grove
The Yoruba people of Nigeria once prayed to their many gods in sacred places in the forest. This grove, honouring the river goddess Osun, is one of the last left.

Kisantu Cathedral, *Democratic Rep. of Congo*

Famous landmarks

Africa boasts breathtaking natural beauty and ancient archaeological wonders. It is home to the rich wildlife of the Serengeti and the thunderous waters of Victoria Falls. And towering minarets, ancient pyramids, and monumental mud-brick architecture reflect the continent's rich cultural history.

● **Great Mosque, Djenné**
Djenné was one of the great cities of the rich Mali Empire, one of Africa's medieval kingdoms, and its mosque was a famous centre of learning. Built of sun-baked bricks made of sand and earth, it was reconstructed in 1907.

FISH RIVER CANYON IS AFRICA'S BIGGEST CANYON: 160 KM (100 MILES)

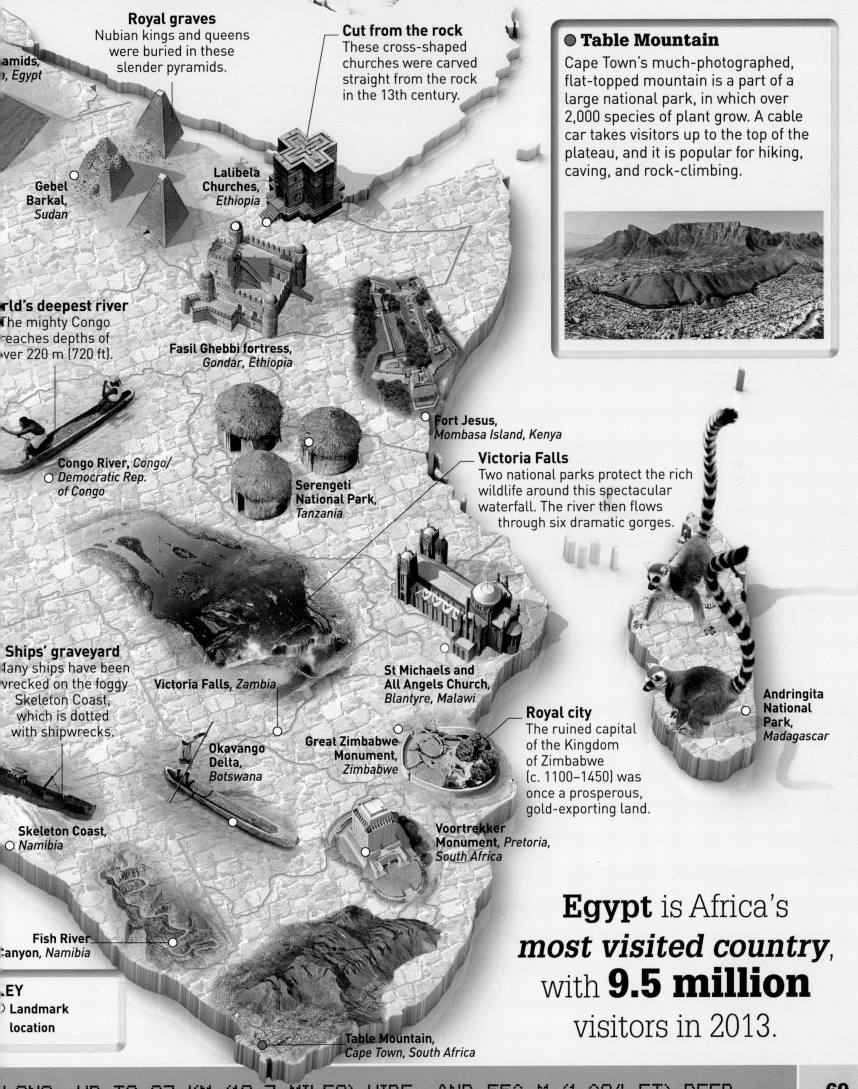

Royal graves
Nubian kings and queens were buried in these slender pyramids.

Cut from the rock
These cross-shaped churches were carved straight from the rock in the 13th century.

● **Table Mountain**
Cape Town's much-photographed, flat-topped mountain is a part of a large national park, in which over 2,000 species of plant grow. A cable car takes visitors up to the top of the plateau, and it is popular for hiking, caving, and rock-climbing.

amids,
a, Egypt

Gebel Barkal, *Sudan*

Lalibela Churches, *Ethiopia*

rld's deepest river
The mighty Congo eaches depths of ver 220 m (720 ft).

Fasil Ghebbi fortress, *Gondar, Ethiopia*

Fort Jesus, *Mombasa Island, Kenya*

Congo River, *Congo/ Democratic Rep. of Congo*

Serengeti National Park, *Tanzania*

Victoria Falls
Two national parks protect the rich wildlife around this spectacular waterfall. The river then flows through six dramatic gorges.

Ships' graveyard
lany ships have been vrecked on the foggy Skeleton Coast, which is dotted with shipwrecks.

Victoria Falls, *Zambia*

St Michaels and All Angels Church, *Blantyre, Malawi*

Andringita National Park, *Madagascar*

Okavango Delta, *Botswana*

Great Zimbabwe Monument, *Zimbabwe*

Royal city
The ruined capital of the Kingdom of Zimbabwe (c. 1100–1450) was once a prosperous, gold-exporting land.

Skeleton Coast, *Namibia*

Voortrekker Monument, *Pretoria, South Africa*

Fish River Canyon, *Namibia*

EY
Landmark location

Table Mountain, *Cape Town, South Africa*

Egypt is Africa's *most visited country*, with **9.5 million** visitors in 2013.

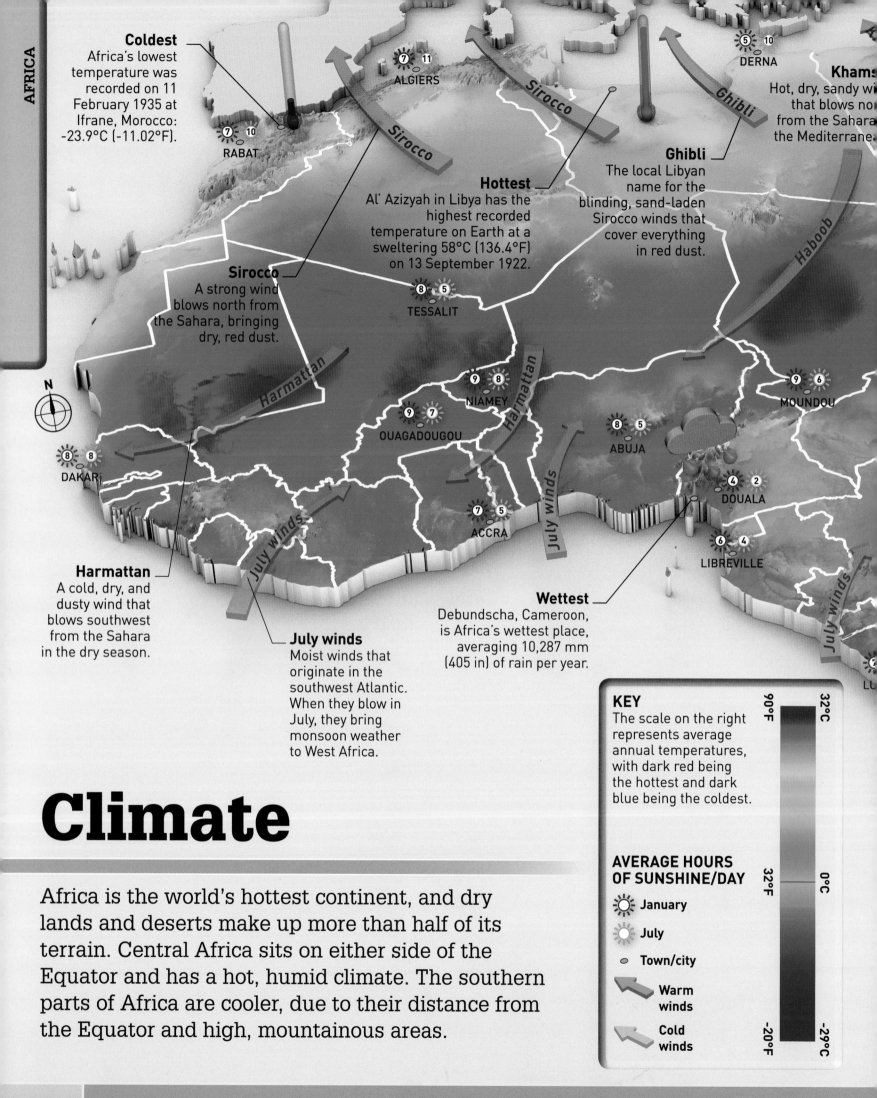

Coldest
Africa's lowest temperature was recorded on 11 February 1935 at Ifrane, Morocco: -23.9°C (-11.02°F).

RABAT

Sirocco
A strong wind blows north from the Sahara, bringing dry, red dust.

ALGIERS

Sirocco

Sirocco

Hottest
Al' Azizyah in Libya has the highest recorded temperature on Earth at a sweltering 58°C (136.4°F) on 13 September 1922.

DERNA

Ghibli

Ghibli
The local Libyan name for the blinding, sand-laden Sirocco winds that cover everything in red dust.

Khams
Hot, dry, sandy wi that blows no from the Sahara the Mediterrane

Haboob

TESSALIT

Harmattan

Harmattan

NIAMEY

OUAGADOUGOU

MOUNDOU

ABUJA

July winds

DOUALA

DAKAR

ACCRA

LIBREVILLE

Harmattan
A cold, dry, and dusty wind that blows southwest from the Sahara in the dry season.

July winds

July winds
Moist winds that originate in the southwest Atlantic. When they blow in July, they bring monsoon weather to West Africa.

Wettest
Debundscha, Cameroon, is Africa's wettest place, averaging 10,287 mm (405 in) of rain per year.

July winds

LU

Climate

Africa is the world's hottest continent, and dry lands and deserts make up more than half of its terrain. Central Africa sits on either side of the Equator and has a hot, humid climate. The southern parts of Africa are cooler, due to their distance from the Equator and high, mountainous areas.

KEY
The scale on the right represents average annual temperatures, with dark red being the hottest and dark blue being the coldest.

90°F — 32°C

32°F — 0°C

-20°F — -29°C

AVERAGE HOURS OF SUNSHINE/DAY

☀ January

☀ July

○ Town/city

⬅ Warm winds

⬅ Cold winds

STORMS HAVE CARRIED SAND FROM THE SAHARA DESERT AS

Sunniest
Aswan, Egypt, is Africa's sunniest place, enjoying an average of 10.6 hours of sunshine per day.

Driest
Wadi Halfa, Sudan, is Africa's driest place, receiving just 2.54 mm (0.1 in) per year.

Haboob

KHARTOUM ⑨ ⑪

DJIBOUTI ⑧ ⑧

ADDIS ABABA ⑨ ②

MOGADISHU ⑨ ⑦

Haboob
...trong winds blow
...outh from the
...ahara during
...inter, causing
...erce sand storms.

KISANGANI ⑦ ⑤

NAIROBI ⑨ ④

DAR ES SALAAM ⑧ ⑧

MZUZU ⑤ ⑦

ANTANANARIVO ⑦ ⑤

...NGO

LUSAKA ⑤ ⑨

HARARE ⑥ ⑨

WINDHOEK ⑨ ⑩

JOHANNESBURG ⑨ ⑨

DURBAN ⑨ ⑨

...outh Africa
...s with most
...untries at
...is latitude in the
...outhern hemisphere,
...e coldest days are from
...ay to July, while summer
...lls from December to February.

CAPE TOWN ⑪ ⑥

Average precipitation

inches	mm
197	5,000
98	2,500
0	0

Scarce rain in the north has helped create the Sahara Desert; the south receives very little rainfall, too. In contrast, Central Africa's rainforests are drenched in more than 4,000 mm (157.5 in) of rain per year. Snow falls in the mountains of Morocco, South Africa, and, more rarely, East Africa.

● **Hot spot**
Dallol, in Ethiopia's Danakil Desert, has the world's highest average temperature: 34.4°C (94°F). The area's few lakes are salt-encrusted and full of sulphur.

Dromedary camel
The Arabian camel has a single hump, which stores fat that the body converts into energy and water.

Deathstalker scorpion
This venomous arachnid feeds at night and lives in cool, shady burrows.

Nile crocodile
An aggressive reptile that surprise-attacks from submerged hiding places.

Ruppell's vulture
Has a powerful, hooked bill for ripping flesh and crushing bone from animal carcasses.

Spotted hyena
Can see in the dark and lives, hunts, and scavenges in female-led groups.

African rock python
Non-venomous but highly aggressive, this is one of the largest snake species, growing up to 7 m (23 ft) in length.

Chimpanzee
Lives in a community and eats mainly fruit and leaves.

African bush elephant
The largest land animal, this elephant lives in grasslands, tropical forests, and semi-deserts.

Lemon shark
This shark favours warm, shallow waters, and uses sensors (called electroreceptors) to detect hidden prey on the ocean floor.

Hippopotamus
This grass-eater is a fast runner, and spends much of its day in the water to cool off.

Whale shark
The largest fish in the world, this shark grows up to 20 m (65.6 ft) and feeds on tiny organisms, such as plankton and krill.

Wildlife

No safari of Africa is complete without seeing the big five – elephant, lion, buffalo, rhino, and leopard – but the African continent is also home to an incredible variety of other animals. Many of these are exclusive to their region, such as the lemur, which can only be found in Madagascar.

BIOMES
Africa is dominated by tropical and sub-tropical grasslands, jungles of tropical broadleaf forest, and dry desert regions.

- Mediterranean
- Tropical broadleaf forest
- Tropical dry broadleaf forest
- Tropical/sub-tropical grassland
- Mountain
- Desert
- Flooded grassland
- Mangrove

Giraffe
Its long legs and neck make it easy to reach leaves at the tops of trees, but hard to bend down to drink.

African wild dog
Hunts in packs to bring down large prey, such as wildebeest.

Serval
Long back legs help this cat jump to snatch birds in flight.

Mass migration
The Serengeti, in East Africa, hosts the world's largest annual migration. More than a million wildebeest move along a circular route on the plain searching for food.

Eastern gorilla
The largest of the primates, it eats mainly fruit and leaves.

African buffalo
Formidably strong with curled horns, females and young live in herds for safety.

Aye aye
One of around 50 species of lemur in Madagascar, it uses its long, thin middle finger to scrape out grubs from trees.

Ostrich
The largest bird and fastest two-legged runner in the world.

Leopard
An incredibly strong cat that can drag large prey up trees to eat.

Lion
The only big cat that lives in groups, its roar can be heard up to 8 km (5 miles) away.

Black rhinoceros
A two-horned rhino with a pointed upper lip that plucks leaves and fruit from bushes.

Warthog
A long-legged pig with four sharp tusks used for defence and foraging.

Tiger shark
A savage scavenger of immense bulk that eats anything it can find in the ocean.

Cheetah
The fastest animal on Earth, it can run at speeds of up to 100 km/h (60 mph).

Black mamba
A highly venomous snake that reveals the black inside its mouth when threatened.

Meerkat
Groups work [tog]ether to look out [for] predators while [f]oraging for food.

Great white shark
This shark is a fierce predator that surprises prey by attacking it from below.

Springbok
[S]mall, speedy antelope that springs high into the air when startled.

THESE EXIST NOWHERE ELSE ON EARTH AND MANY ARE ENDANGERED.

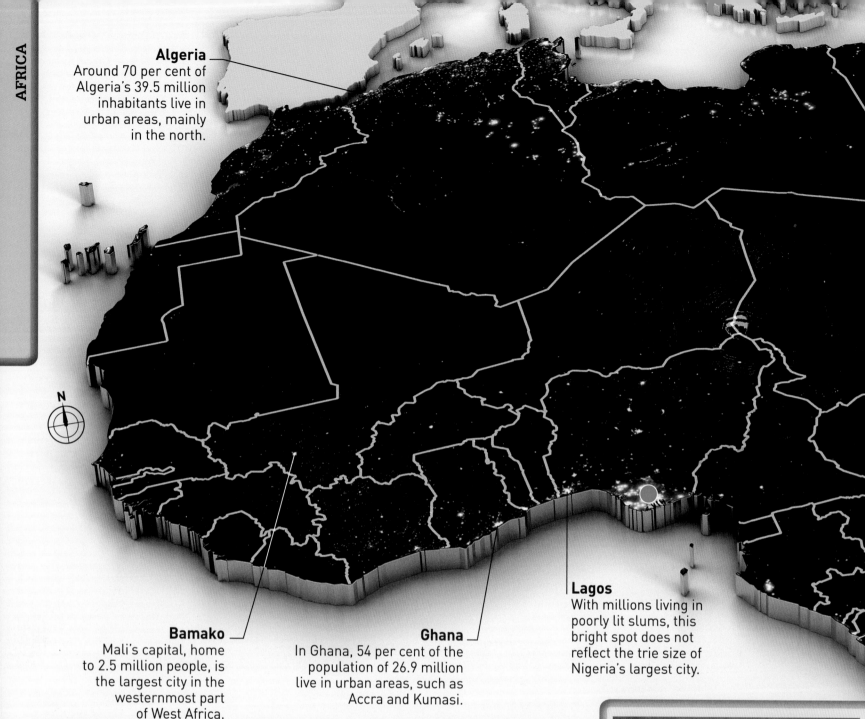

Algeria
Around 70 per cent of
Algeria's 39.5 million
inhabitants live in
urban areas, mainly
in the north.

Bamako
Mali's capital, home
to 2.5 million people, is
the largest city in the
westernmost part
of West Africa.

Ghana
In Ghana, 54 per cent of the
population of 26.9 million
live in urban areas, such as
Accra and Kumasi.

Lagos
With millions living in
poorly lit slums, this
bright spot does not
reflect the trie size of
Nigeria's largest city.

By night

The speed at which cities grow in population
is very high in Africa. But here, not all densely
populated places show up at night – poorer areas
do not have street lights, lit-up shop windows,
or even electric indoor lights. Most dark areas,
however, are desert, jungle, or savannah.

● **Niger Delta oil fields**
Much of the strong glow in
Nigeria's Niger Delta comes from
the many oil fields, with their
open gas flares, big refineries,
and busy ports.

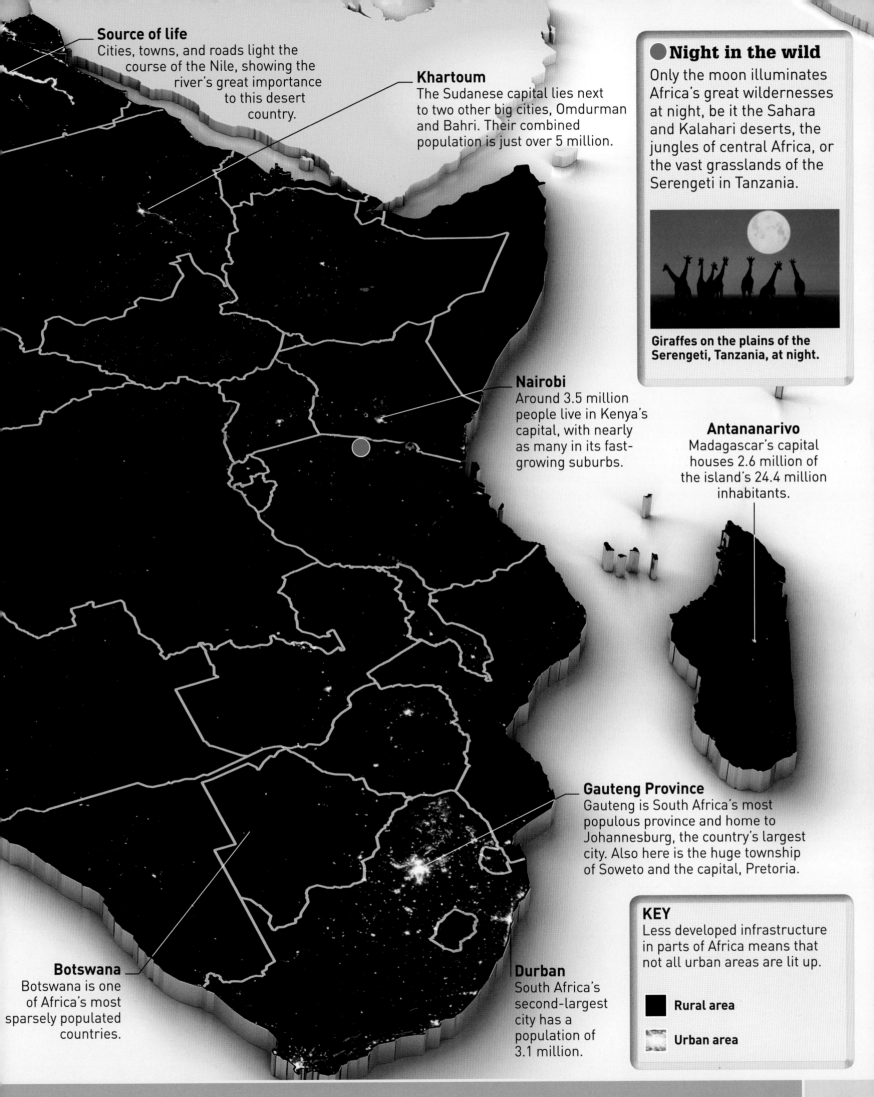

Source of life
Cities, towns, and roads light the course of the Nile, showing the river's great importance to this desert country.

Khartoum
The Sudanese capital lies next to two other big cities, Omdurman and Bahri. Their combined population is just over 5 million.

Night in the wild
Only the moon illuminates Africa's great wildernesses at night, be it the Sahara and Kalahari deserts, the jungles of central Africa, or the vast grasslands of the Serengeti in Tanzania.

Giraffes on the plains of the Serengeti, Tanzania, at night.

Nairobi
Around 3.5 million people live in Kenya's capital, with nearly as many in its fast-growing suburbs.

Antananarivo
Madagascar's capital houses 2.6 million of the island's 24.4 million inhabitants.

Gauteng Province
Gauteng is South Africa's most populous province and home to Johannesburg, the country's largest city. Also here is the huge township of Soweto and the capital, Pretoria.

Botswana
Botswana is one of Africa's most sparsely populated countries.

Durban
South Africa's second-largest city has a population of 3.1 million.

KEY
Less developed infrastructure in parts of Africa means that not all urban areas are lit up.

■ Rural area

▨ Urban area

EUROPE

Europe from space
The European continent lies in the northern hemisphere and has an eastern land border with Asia. The distinctive "boot" of Italy is clearly visible in this image.

Countries and borders

The borders of European countries have changed many times over history, as conquering armies advanced and defeated ones retreated. In the 20th century, two world wars shook the continent, and conflict and political change continue to shape the continent's borders.

United Kingdom
It is formed of England, Scotland, Wales, and Northern Ireland.

Norwegian Sea

FINLA

SWEDEN

HELSI

NORWAY

STOCKHOLM

OSLO

Gothenburg

Baltic S

Aalborg

COPENHAGEN

Gda

DENMARK

Poz

ICELAND
REYKJAVÍK

ATLANTIC OCEAN

Faroe Islands
(to Denmark)

North Sea

Hamburg

BERLIN

Edinburgh

NETHERLANDS

GERMANY

Belfast

UNITED

AMSTERDAM

Düsseldorf

PRA

DUBLIN

Manchester

BRUSSELS

Frankfurt am Main

IRELAND

KINGDOM

BELGIUM

Stuttgart

Salzb

Cardiff

LONDON

LUXEMBOURG

Munich

AUS

LUXEMBOURG

British Isles

PARIS

LIECHTENSTEIN

VADUZ

BERN

Ven

Rennes

SWITZERLAND

Andorra
The small principality was formed in 1278. It is bordered by France to the north and by Spain to the south.

FRANCE

Milan

Lyon

Turin

ITAL

Bordeaux

Bay of Biscay

MONACO

Marseille

Corsica

ANDORRA
LA VELLA

A Coruña

Bilbao

ANDORRA

Barcelona

Porto

Zaragoza

Sardinia

MADRID

Valencia

Balearic Islands

PORTUGAL

SPAIN

LISBON

Mediterranea

Seville

Málaga

AFRICA

Gibraltar
(to UK)

FAST FACTS

Total land area:
10,498,000 sq km
(4,053,300 sq miles)

Total population:
743 million

Number of countries: 46

Largest country:
Russian Federation
(European section)
– 3,955,818 sq km
(1,527,350 sq miles)

Smallest country:
Vatican City – 0.44 sq km
(0.17 sq miles)

Largest country population:
Russian Federation
(European section) –
110 million

THE VATICAN CITY, THE WORLD'S SMALLEST COUNTRY (POPULATION:

Approximately **25 per cent** of the Russian Federation lies **within Europe**; the rest is in Asia.

RUSSIAN

FEDERATION

Perm'

Archangel

Samara

Nizhniy Novgorod

St Petersburg

MOSCOW

Volograd

Astrakhan'

TONIA

LATVIA

A

VILNIUS

MINSK

Kharkiv

Rostov-na-Donu

THUANIA

Homyel'

KIEV

Donets'k

BELARUS

UKRAINE

WARSAW

Simferopol

OLAND

L'viv

MOLDOVA

Odesa

Crimea

Krakow

CHISINAU

ECH
UBLIC

SLOVAKIA

Cluj-Napoca

Black Sea

NA

BRATISLAVA

BUDAPEST

ROMANIA

BUCHAREST

HUNGARY

UBLJANA

BELGRADE

Burgas

Istanbul

ZAGREB

BOSNIA
& HERZEGOVINA

SERBIA

KOSOVO
(disputed)

BULGARIA

TURKEY

VENIA

SARAJEVO

PRISTINA

SOFIA

ASIA

CROATIA

MONTENEGRO

RINO

PODGORICA

MACEDONIA

SKOPJE

OME

TIRANA

VATICAN CITY

Naples

ALBANIA

GREECE

ATHENS

Ionian
Sea

Irakleio

yrrhenian
Sea

Crete

Palermo

Sicily

VALLETTA

e a

MALTA

The Russian Federation
Russia is a vast federation (union) of states that crosses two continents, Europe and Asia. Until 1991, it was a bigger nation, called the Soviet Union, which then split into 15 new states. Of these, Estonia, Latvia, Lithuania, Belarus, Ukraine, and Moldova are now independent countries in Europe.

KEY
● Capital city
● Major city

Turkey
Geographically, 3 per cent of Turkey lies within Europe. The majority of the country is in Asia.

EUROPEAN UNION
The formation of the European Economic Community (now the European Union) in 1957 saw many European countries move towards a closer political and economic union.

Balkan countries
Slovenia, Croatia, Bosnia-Herzegovina, Macedonia, Montenegro, and Serbia used to be in a country called Yugoslavia. They became separate countries between 1991 and 2006 following years of conflict.

KEY
6 original members, 1957
9 further members, 1973–95
10 further members, 2004
2 further members, 2007
1 further member, 2013

AROUND 1,000), BECAME AN INDEPENDENT STATE IN 1929.

Landscape

Despite its small size, the continent of Europe has an incredibly diverse landscape. To the northwest, east, and south, it is enclosed by mountains. In between, lies the North European Plain, which stretches 4,000 km (2,485 miles) from eastern England to the Ural Mountains in Russia.

Novaya Zemlya

Barents Sea

Ko Penin

Kölen

Norwegian Sea

Gulf of Bothnia

ATLANTIC OCEAN

Iceland

Faroe Islands

Shetland Islands

a

Vänern

Vättern

Jutland

Baltic S

Orkney Islands

Outer Hebrides

North Sea

N o r t

Ireland

Britain
④

British Isles

English Channel

Seine

Mont Blanc 4,808 m 15,780 ft

A l p s

Rhône

Loire

Appennin

Bay of Biscay

Pyrenees

Corsica

Ebro

Douro

Iberian Peninsula

Sardinia

Balearic Islands

M e d i t e r r a n e a

A F R I C A

FAST FACTS

① Highest point:
Mount Elbrus, Russia –
5,642 m (18,510 ft)

② Longest river:
Volga, Russia –
3,688 km (2,291 miles)

③ Largest lake:
Lake Ladoga, Russia –
18,390 sq km
(7,100 sq miles)

④ Largest island:
Britain (England,
Wales, and Scotland) –
229,848 sq km
(88,745 sq miles)

③

Europe's largest lake, Ladoga lies close to the city of St Petersburg, in Russia.

EUROPE HAS A HIGHER RATIO OF COAST TO LANDMASS

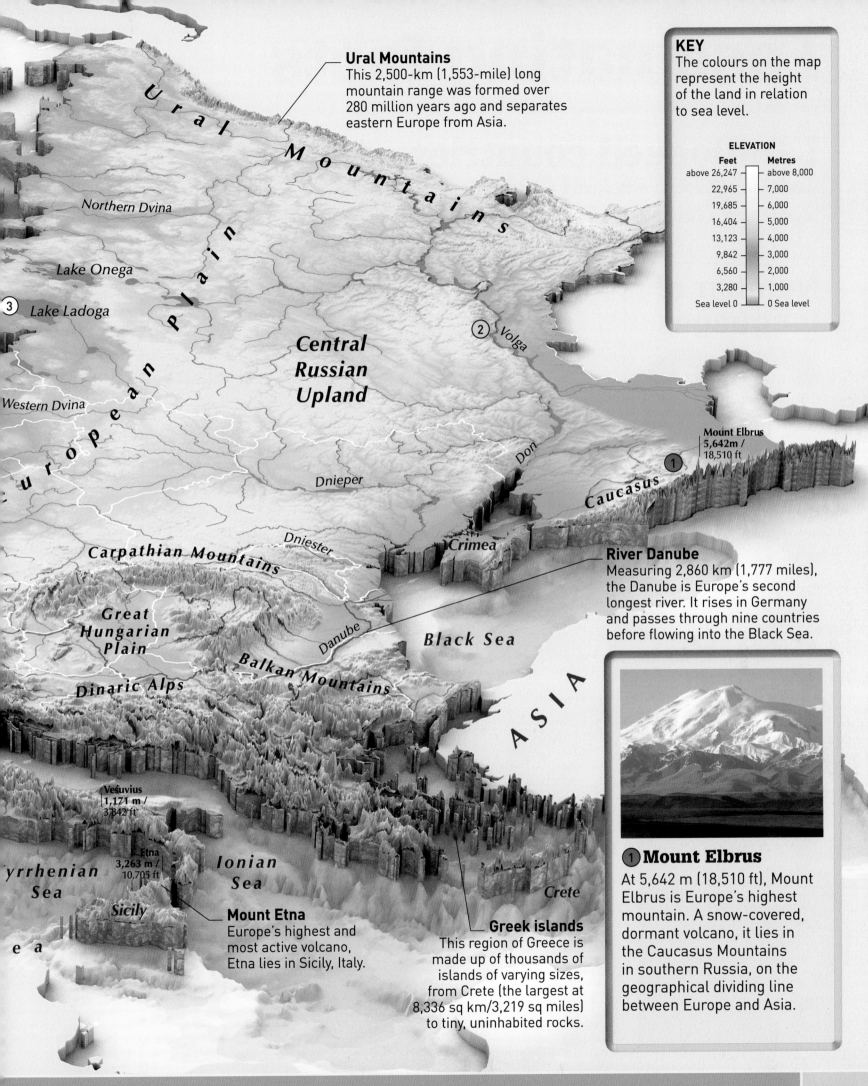

Ural Mountains
This 2,500-km (1,553-mile) long mountain range was formed over 280 million years ago and separates eastern Europe from Asia.

U r a l M o u n t a i n s

Northern Dvina

Lake Onega

③ *Lake Ladoga*

Western Dvina

Central Russian Upland

② *Volga*

E u r o p e a n   P l a i n

Dnieper

Don

Mount Elbrus
5,642m /
18,510 ft

①

Caucasus

Dniester

Carpathian Mountains

Crimea

Danube

River Danube
Measuring 2,860 km (1,777 miles), the Danube is Europe's second longest river. It rises in Germany and passes through nine countries before flowing into the Black Sea.

Great Hungarian Plain

Black Sea

Dinaric Alps

Balkan Mountains

A S I A

Vesuvius
1,171 m /
3,842 ft

yrrhenian Sea

Etna /
3,263 m /
10,705 ft

Ionian Sea

Crete

Sicily

e a

Mount Etna
Europe's highest and most active volcano, Etna lies in Sicily, Italy.

Greek islands
This region of Greece is made up of thousands of islands of varying sizes, from Crete (the largest at 8,336 sq km/3,219 sq miles) to tiny, uninhabited rocks.

KEY
The colours on the map represent the height of the land in relation to sea level.

ELEVATION

Feet		Metres
above 26,247		above 8,000
22,965		7,000
19,685		6,000
16,404		5,000
13,123		4,000
9,842		3,000
6,560		2,000
3,280		1,000
Sea level 0		0 Sea level

① **Mount Elbrus**
At 5,642 m (18,510 ft), Mount Elbrus is Europe's highest mountain. A snow-covered, dormant volcano, it lies in the Caucasus Mountains in southern Russia, on the geographical dividing line between Europe and Asia.

THAN ANY OTHER CONTINENT OR SUBCONTINENT.

Fascinating facts

Landlocked countries – 14

Andorra ▪ Austria ▪ **Belarus** ▪ Czech Republic ▪ **Hungary** ▪ Liechtenstein ▪ **Luxembourg** ▪ Macedonia ▪ **Moldova** ▪ San Marino ▪ **Serbia** ▪ Slovakia ▪ **Switzerland** ▪ Vatican City

Number of languages

39

There are 39 official European languages and many more regional languages and dialects.

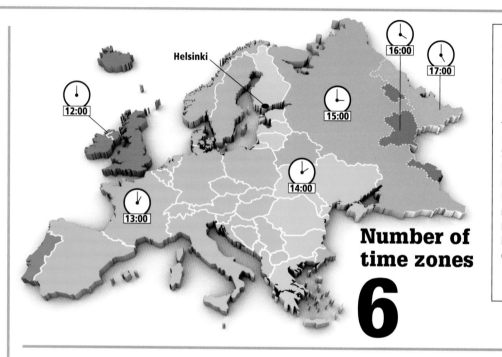

Helsinki

12:00

16:00

17:00

15:00

14:00

13:00

Number of time zones

6

The world is split into 39 time zones. Most are set whole hours ahead or behind Coordinated Universal Time (UCT) – the time at the Greenwich Meridian in London, UK. Some, however, are whole hours plus 30 or 45 minutes ahead or behind UCT. Therefore, on this map, if it was 12:00 in London, it would be 14:00 in Helsinki, Finland (2 hours ahead of UCT).

Deepest lake

Hornindalsvattnet, Norway – **514 m (1,686 ft)**

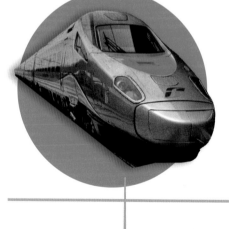

Fastest train

Europe's fastest train is the **Frecciarossa 1000** in **Italy**, which can reach speeds of up to **400 km/h (249 mph)**

Tallest buildings

Federation Tower
Moscow, Russia
373.7 m (1,226 ft)

OKO: South Tower
Moscow, Russia
354.1 m (1,162 ft)

Mercury City Tower
Moscow, Russia
338.8 m (1,112 ft)

The Shard
London, United Kingdom
309.6 m (1,016 ft)

Eurasia
Moscow, Russia
308.9 m (1,013 ft)

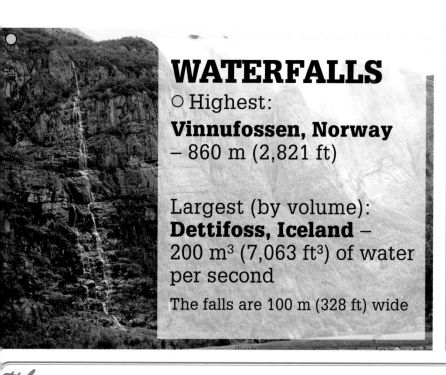

WATERFALLS
○ Highest:
Vinnufossen, Norway – 860 m (2,821 ft)

Largest (by volume):
Dettifoss, Iceland – 200 m³ (7,063 ft³) of water per second

The falls are 100 m (328 ft) wide

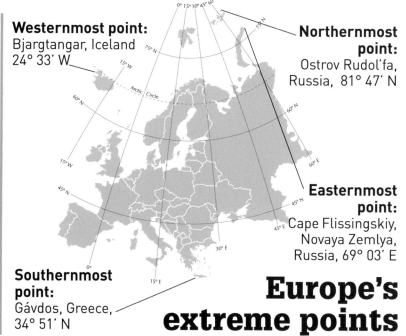

Westernmost point: Bjargtangar, Iceland 24° 33' W

Northernmost point: Ostrov Rudol'fa, Russia, 81° 47' N

Easternmost point: Cape Flissingskiy, Novaya Zemlya, Russia, 69° 03' E

Southernmost point: Gávdos, Greece, 34° 51' N

Europe's extreme points

 Busiest airport Heathrow Airport, London, UK: **74,985 million passengers per year**

Longest tunnels

 Railway tunnel Gotthard Base Tunnel, Switzerland – 57.09 km (35.5 miles)

 Metro line Serpukhovsko line, Moscow, Russia – 41.5 km (25.8 miles)

 Road tunnel Laerdal, Norway – 24.53 km (15.2 miles)

Longest bridge
Vasco da Gama, Lisbon, Portugal **17.185 km (10.68 miles)**

Biggest glacier
Severny Island ice cap – northern island of the Novaya Zemlya archipelago in Russia – **20,500 sq km (7,915 sq miles)**

Longest coastline

Norway
25,148 km (15,626 miles)

Highest mountains

1. Mount Elbrus Russia 5,642 m (18,510 ft)

2. Dychtau Russia 5,204 m (17,073 ft)

3. Mont Blanc France 4,808 m (15,774 ft)

4. Dafourspitze Switzerland 4,634 m (15,203 ft)

5. Zumsteinspitze Switzerland 4,563 m (14,970 ft)

Most active volcano
Mount Etna, Italy

Highest bridge
Millau Viaduct, France – bridge deck is **270 m (886 ft)** above the ground

Population

Murmansk, Russia
Murmansk, Russia
The largest city north of the Arctic Circle. It has 299,000 inhabitants.

Europe is the world's second-most densely populated continent (after Asia), with an average of 73 people per sq km (188 per sq mile). The majority of Europe's population live in the northern half of the continent.

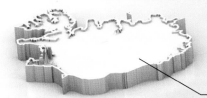

Iceland
This island of volcanoes and icy wilderness has the lowest population density in Europe – 3 people per sq km (8 people per sq mile).

Norway
Scandinavia's most sparsely populated country, with 16 people per sq km (42 people per sq mile).

Netherlands
With a population of 17 million, this is one of Europe's most densely populated nations, at 409 people per sq km (1,060 per sq mile).

Europe's largest cities
The list below is based on the number of people living inside a city's boundaries.

1. **Istanbul, Turkey –** 14.7 million

2. **Moscow, Russia – 12.3 million**

3. **London, United Kingdom –** 8.7 million

4. **St Petersburg, Russia –** 5.2 million

5. **Berlin, Germany – 3.6 million**

6. **Madrid, Spain – 3.1 million**

7. **Kiev, Ukraine – 2.9 million**

8. **Rome, Italy – 2.87 million**

9. **Paris, France – 2.2 million**

10. **Minsk, Belarus – 1.9 million**

The Eiffel Tower dominates the skyline of Paris, France's most populous city.

Madrid
Population density in Spain's capital is 5,390 people per sq km (14,000 per sq mile), almost as high as that of London.

Monaco
The small principality is the world's mos densely populat nation, with 15,2 people per sq k (39,602 per sq m

OF THE WORLD'S 10 MOST DENSELY POPULATED LOCATIONS, FOUR

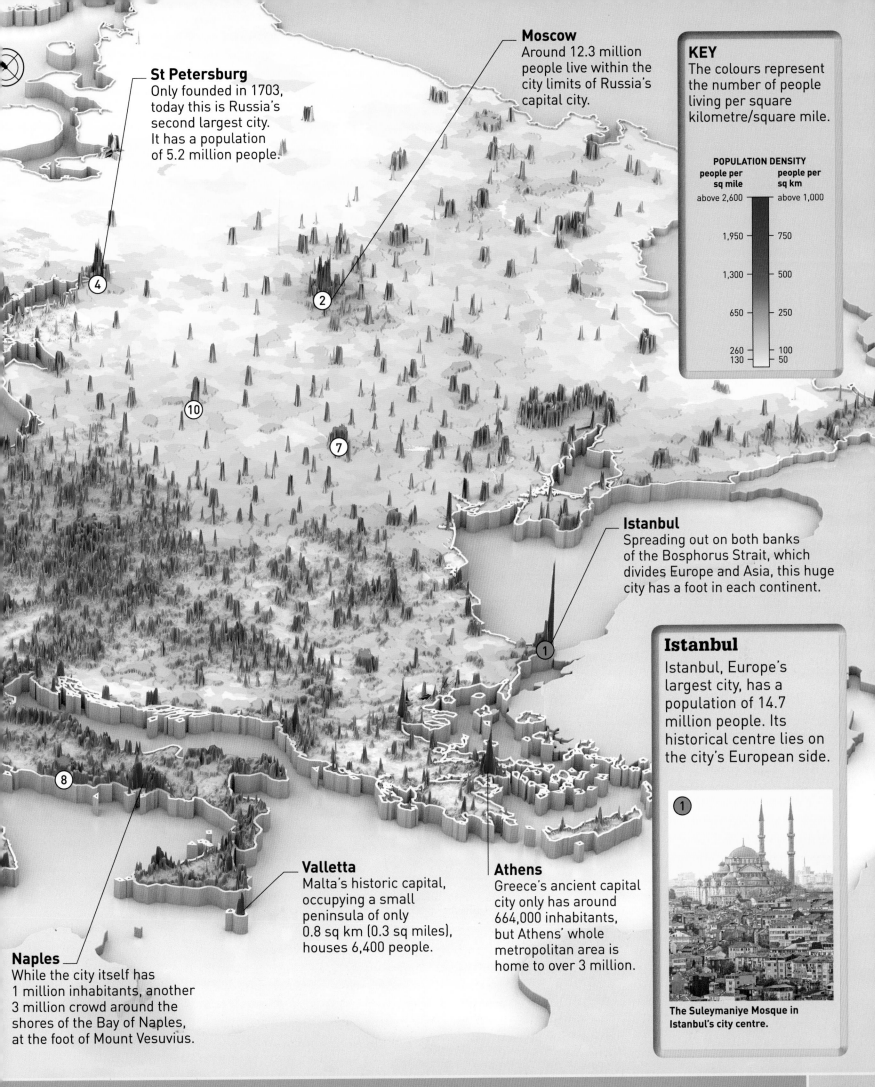

St Petersburg
Only founded in 1703, today this is Russia's second largest city. It has a population of 5.2 million people.

Moscow
Around 12.3 million people live within the city limits of Russia's capital city.

POPULATION DENSITY

people per sq mile	people per sq km
above 2,600	above 1,000
1,950	750
1,300	500
650	250
260	100
130	50

Istanbul
Spreading out on both banks of the Bosphorus Strait, which divides Europe and Asia, this huge city has a foot in each continent.

Istanbul
Istanbul, Europe's largest city, has a population of 14.7 million people. Its historical centre lies on the city's European side.

The Suleymaniye Mosque in Istanbul's city centre.

Valletta
Malta's historic capital, occupying a small peninsula of only 0.8 sq km (0.3 sq miles), houses 6,400 people.

Athens
Greece's ancient capital city only has around 664,000 inhabitants, but Athens' whole metropolitan area is home to over 3 million.

Naples
While the city itself has 1 million inhabitants, another 3 million crowd around the shores of the Bay of Naples, at the foot of Mount Vesuvius.

Highest road
At 2,764 m (9,068 ft), Col de l'Iseran, France, is only accesible by car in summer. Tour de France cyclists have struggled over it several times.

Biggest glacier
The Aletsch glacier, Switzerland, measures over 900 m (2,950 ft) at its thickest, and is 117 sq km (45 sq miles) in size, but it is melting every year.

Mont Blanc
On the border between France and Italy, the "white mountain" is topped by a permanent cap of snow and ice. A road tunnel runs through its base.

SWITZERLAND

BERN

Lake Geneva

Geneva

Pennine Alps

A

Leponti

Po

Turin

Southernmost Alps
The Maritime Alps straddle the France-Italy border and run all the way down to the sea.

French Alps

Cottian Alps

FRANCE

Maritime Alps

Artificial lake
The Lac Serre-Ponçon, one of Europe's biggest artificial lakes, was created from 1955–61 to prevent flooding. It covers 28 sq km (10.8 sq miles) and is up to 90 m (295 ft) deep.

French Alps
This range sits within France and contains Mont Blanc.

THE ALPS ARE HOME TO 14 MILLION PEOPLE AND 120 MILLION

GERMANY

Munich

AUSTRIA

S

Ips

Dolomites

Piave

Brenta Venice

Gulf of Venice

Adige

Lake Garda

Mincio

Po

Reno

Bologna

Appenines
These mountains run the
length of Italy, and most
of the country's rivers
have their source here.

Maggiore

Milan

Adda

P o   V a l l e y

Ticino

Po

I T A L Y

A p p e n i n e s

Po river
eginning in the Cottian
ps, the mighty Po river
fed by several smaller
rivers coming down
from the Pennine and
Lepontine Alps and
the Dolomites.

Genoa

*Gulf of
Genoa*

M e d i t e r r a n e a n   S e a

Lake Garda
At 367 sq km
(142 sq miles), Garda
is the largest of
Italy's great Alpine
lakes. It reaches a
depth of 346 m
(1,135 ft) at its
narrow northern end.

The Alps

The Alps are the highest and most extensive
mountain range in western Europe. Shaped
like a crescent, they stretch across eight
countries for 1,200 km (750 miles) and are 200 km
(125 miles) wide at their broadest point. Over 100
peaks are in excess of 4,000 m (13,123 ft), the highest
of which is Mont Blanc, on the France-Italy border.

HIGHEST PEAKS
With the exception of Mont
Blanc, the Alps' highest peaks
are all situated in Switzerland.

△ **Mont Blanc** 4,808 m (15,774 ft)

△ **Monte Rosa** 4,634 m (15,203 ft)

△ **Dom** 4,545 m (14,911 ft)

△ **Weisshorn** 4,506 m (14,783 ft)

△ **Matterhorn** 4,478 m (14,692 ft)

Famous landmarks

From prehistoric monuments and Roman ruins to medieval town centres, Gothic cathedrals, and Baroque palaces, Europe has a wealth of architectural treasures from across the ages. Some of its most famous landmarks are natural formations, often protected as national parks.

Thingvellir National Park, *Iceland*

Drottningholm Palace, *Sweden*

Urnes Stave Church, *Norway*

United Kingdom

The 29 UNESCO heritage sites in England, Scotland, Wales, and Northern Ireland include Stone Age monuments, castles, and feats of Victorian engineering.

Edinburgh Castle, *Scotland*

Kronborg Castle, *Helsingør, Denmark*

Giant's Causeway, *Northern Ireland*

Kinderdijk-Elshout Windmills, *Netherlands*

Big Ben, *London, England*

Stonehenge, *England*

Charlottenburg Pala *Berlin, Germany*

Landscapes

Europe has 468 national parks. Some are precious habitats or areas of natural beauty, while others contain particular geological formations.

Aachen Cathedral, *Germany*

Eiffel Tower, *Paris, France*

Brú na Bóinne, *Ireland*

Hôtel de Ville, *Brussels, Belgium*

○ Iceland's Thingvellir National Park lies at the meeting point between the North American and Eurasian plates.

France

Among France's many famous landmarks, 42 are UNESCO World Heritage Sites.

Chartres Cathedral, *France*

Rhaetian Railway, *Switzerland*

Palais des Papes, *Avignon, France*

Leaning Tow of Pisa, I

Sagrada Familia, *Barcelona, Spain*

○ Giant's Causeway, Northern Ireland, is made of basalt columns in different formations, some like giant honeycombs.

Toledo Cathedral, *Spain*

Torre de Belem, *Lisbon, Portugal*

Moorish Alhambra

Many of Spain's landmarks show the country's Arabic heritage, such as the Alhamb palace and gardens in Granac

Alhambra, *Granada, Spain*

OF EUROPE'S MANY LANDMARKS, 453 ARE DESIGNATED UNESCO WORLD

Petjävesi Wooden Church, *Finland*

St Isaac's Cathedral, *St Petersburg, Russia*

Onion-dome churches
Onion domes top many churches in central and eastern Europe, the most famous of which is the colourful St Basil's Cathedral in Moscow.

St Basil's Cathedral, *Moscow, Russia*

St Nicholas' Church, *Tallinn, Estonia*

Vilnius Cathedral, *Vilnius, Lithuania*

Mir Castle Complex, *Belarus*

St Sophia Cathedral, *Kiev, Ukraine*

France is the *most visited* country **in the world**, with over **85 million** tourists per year.

Historic Centre of Riga, *Latvia*

Historic Centre of Krakow, *Poland*

Levoča, *Prešov Region, Slovakia*

Struve Geodetic Arc, *Rudi, Moldova*

gue hedral, *ch ublic*

Stephansdom Quarter, *Vienna, Austria*

Matthias Church, *Budapest, Hungary*

Wooden Churches of Maramureş, *Romania*

Stari Ras and Sopoćani, *Serbia*

Old Bridge, *Mostar, Bosnia & Herz*

Prehistoric Dwellings, *Ljubljansko Barje, Slovenia*

Rila Monastery, *Bulgaria*

Buildings
Europe's architectural landmarks, whether in ruins, reconstructed, or in their original glory, all tell fascinating tales of the continent's history and its people.

Palace of Diocletian, *Split, Croatia*

Parthenon, *Athens, Greece*

Butrint, *Chaonia, Albania*

Meteora, *Greece*

Colosseum, *Rome, Italy*

○ The historic city centre of Riga, Latvia, is a mix of fine medieval buildings and some of the world's best Art Nouveau architecture.

Pompeii, *Italy*

Kotor Old Town, *Montenegro*

Church of St John at Kaneo, *Ohrid, Macedonia*

Duomo, *Florence, Italy*

Valley of Temples, *Agrigento, Italy*

Ancient Greek ruins
The Valley of the Temples in Agrigento, Sicily, is one of many ancient Greek sites dotted around the Mediterranean.

● Meteora, Greece, features a breathtaking group of monasteries perched on vertical cliffs. Only six of the original 24 remain today.

KEY
○ Landmark location

Climate

Europe's climate varies from subtropical in the south to polar in the north. Western and north-western parts have a mild, generally humid climate, while central and eastern Europe has a humid climate with cool summers.

Polar easterlies
Prevailing winds that bring dry, cold air southwards from the North Pole.

Polar easterlies

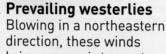

Prevailing westerlies
Blowing in a northeastern direction, these winds bring warm air to western parts of Europe.

Prevailing westerlies

Prevailing westerlies

Prevailing westerlies

Cloudiest
Glasgow, in the United Kingdom, is Europe's cloudiest city. It averages only 1,203 hours of sunshine a year.

REYKJAVIK ① ⑤

FAROE ISLANDS ⓪ ④

HELS ①

STOCKHOLM ① ⑩

OSLO ① ⑦

GLASGOW ② ⑤

COPENHAGEN ① ⑧

BERLIN ① ⑦

AMSTERDAM ① ⑥

PRA ②

LONDON ② ⑥

BRUSSELS ② ⑥

LUXEMBOURG ① ⑦

Föhn

PARIS ② ⑧

BERN ② ⑦

VADUZ ② ⑥

MILAN ② ⑩

LYON ② ⑧

Mistral

BORDEAUX ③ ⑨

MONACO ⑤ ⑪

Mistral
A strong, cold wind that blows hardest in winter and spring.

BARCELONA ③ ⑨

CAGLI

④

MADRID ⑤ ⑮

Hottest
The highest temperature recorded in Europe is 50°C (122°F), in Seville, Spain, on 4 August 1881.

Sirocco

Sirocco

Sirocco winds
Hot air from Africa creates storms over the sea, bringing cloud, fog, and rain to northern Mediterranean locations.

LISBON ⑤ ⑬

ON 7 JULY 1889, 205.7 MM (8.1 IN) OF RAIN FELL AT THE CITY OF

Coldest
The lowest temperature ever recorded in Europe is -55°C (-67°F), in Ust'Shchugor, northern Russia.

Annual precipitation
This map shows the difference in the average amounts of precipitation (snow and rain) that falls across Europe in a year; the darkest blue marking the highest amounts. Westerly winds bring more rain to the western coastal regions, while the Alps get high amounts in winter, usually in the form of snow.

inches		mm
197		5,000
98		2,500
0		0

ST PETERSBURG

MOSCOW

LINN

RGA

VILNIUS

MINSK

WARSAW

KIEV

CHISINAU

BUDAPEST

BELGRADE

BUCHAREST

SOFIA

ISTANBUL

VIENNA

ZAGREB

SARAJEVO

SKOPJE

TIRANA

ATHENS

ROME

MESSINA

VALLETTA

ASTRAKHAN

Driest
Astrakhan, Russia, is Europe's driest city. On average, only 62.6 mm (2.5 in) of rain falls there per year.

Bora winds
Cold, typically dry, and often gusty winds blow down from the mountains on the eastern side of the Adriatic Sea.

Etesian
Prevailing summer winds blow over large areas of Greece.

Wettest
Crkvica, in Bosnia-Herzegovina, is Europe's wettest place. It gets on average 4,648 mm (183 in) of rain a year.

Sunniest
Malta's capital, Valletta, averages 2,957 hours of sunshine a year, making it Europe's sunniest city.

ese warm, strong ds descend from eastern Alps.

Bora

Etesian

Sirocco

KEY
The scale on the right represents average annual temperatures, with dark red being the hottest and dark blue being the coldest.

90°F — 32°C

32°F — 0°C

-20°F — -29°C

AVERAGE HOURS OF SUNSHINE/DAY

☀ January

☀ July

◦ Town/city

⬆ Warm winds

⬆ Cold winds

Wildlife

In densely populated Europe there is not much wilderness left for animals to thrive in, but nature reserves and some species' ability to adapt mean that the continent's wildlife is still surprisingly varied.

Humpback whale
In winter, Arctic waters provide rich feeding grounds for these migrating whales.

Reindeer
Both male a female reind have antlers

Eurasian lynx
Large padded paws prevent this big cat from sinking through the snow.

Arctic fox
Thick, white winter fur keeps this fox warm and camouflaged in snow and ice.

Elk
This giant of the forest is commonly seen in Scandinavia and the Baltic states.

Capercail
A bird famou its spectacu courting ritu

Red deer
Scotland has its own subspecies of this large deer, which is common throughout the continent.

Roe deer
Small and graceful, this deer is widespread throughout Europe.

Irish hare
Modern farming practices threaten this shy, nocturnal creature.

Grey wolf
The largest of the dog family, wolves live in family packs in isolated, forested areas of Europe.

Basking shark
To feed, this gigantic shark simply keeps its mouth wide open as it swims.

Badger
Big groups live in setts (tunnels and underground chambers).

Pine marten
Hollow trees make good homes for this member of the weasel family.

Alpine marmot
These rodents hibernate in burrows for up to nine months.

Golden eagle
This huge raptor picks and patrols huge territories in less populated areas across Europe.

Pyrenean chamois
Close to extinction, as its skin was used for chamois gloves and polishing cloths, the numbers have recovered.

European bee eater
Male birds offer the best insect morsels to the female during courtship.

Barbary macaque
A 300-strong colony of Barbary macaques lives on the Rock of Gibraltar.

Iberian lynx
Only around 400 remain of the endangered Spanish lynx.

Eurasian brown bear
Found in Scandinavia and eastern Europe, these omnivores love berries and fresh fish.

Wolverine
Incredibly fierce, this predator hunts in the tundra and northern forests.

White-tailed eagle
Once almost extinct, this enormous bird now soars across northern Europe.

Eurasian otter
This web-footed otter catches fish in lakes, rivers, and ponds all over Europe.

European polecat
This hunter produces a stinky smell to defend its territory.

European bison
Hunted near to extinction in the 1920s, the bison has been reintroduced to the wild.

Red fox
Common across the European countryside, this opportunist now also thrives in cities.

Changing habitats
Many of the forests that once covered most of Europe have been replaced by farmland, towns and villages, and roads. Wild animals lost their habitats and were hunted, many to near extinction, but today some protected species, such as the grey wolf, are slowly spreading again.

European wild cat
Striped, bushy-tailed, and larger than domestic cats, this rare species lives in southern and central forests.

Golden jackal
A hunter and scavenger, it has started to spread north and west from the Balkans.

BIOMES
In the north, the wide tundra and dense boreal forests and taiga provide good shelter for hardy animals. The temperate forest and grasslands and dry, warm Mediterranean biomes of the rest of Europe make for great habitats for a variety of species, but many are threatened by the impact of human activity.

- Ice
- Tundra
- Boreal forest/Taiga
- Temperate broadleaf forest
- Temperate coniferous forest
- Temperate grassland
- Mediterranean
- Desert

Wild boar
These large, bristly pigs are abundant in southern Europe.

Greater flamingo
Mudflats and coastal lagoons are home to these noisy, pink birds.

Common dolphin
These playful, sociable dolphins travel the Mediterranean in big groups.

Mediterranean monk seal
One of the world's most endangered sea mammals, this seal breeds in underwater caves.

MAMMAL LEFT, OF WHICH 219 LIVE ON LAND.

By night

This satellite image of Europe at night shows where people live. The west of the continent is densely populated; the north and east are relatively uninhabited.

Scandinavia
The relatively small populations of the large Scandinavian countries are concentrated in the main southern coastal cities.

Iceland
Reykjavík is almost the only bright spot, and is home to two-thirds of the country's population.

Northwest England
The triangle formed by the cities of Liverpool, Manchester, and Birmingham is densely populated.

Mega metropolitan area
Urban areas of Belgium, the Netherlands, Luxembourg, and Germany's Rhine-Ruhr form a continuous built-up zone.

London
Europe's third-largest city has a population density of 5,518 people per sq km (14,290 per sq mile).

● **Urban Monaco**
The small principality of Monaco, squeezed into an area of only 2 sq km (0.78 sq miles), is all city. Every one of its 30,581 inhabitants lives in an urban environment.

Paris
About 20 per cent of France's 62.8 million inhabitants live in the Paris metropolitan area.

Industrial hub
Milan and Turin, two of Italy's major industrial an economic centr are home to combined 6.5 million peopl

Lisbon
Just over one-quarter (26.2 per cent) of Portugal's 10.8 million inhabitants live in the metropolitan area of Lisbon.

Madrid
Madrid is Spain's largest metropolitan area and 6.3 million people live here.

ALBANIA IS THE COUNTRY WITH THE FASTEST GROWING

KEY
Illuminated areas reflect urban, built-up zones and roads, in contrast to rural regions.

■ Rural area

▨ Urban area

Moscow
Russia's capital and its many sprawling suburbs are home to 17 million people.

Romania
The country's population is almost evenly split between urban and rural areas, with just over half living in towns and cities.

● **The empty north**
Northern Europe's great swathes of forests and tundra are almost unpopulated, except for some small villages and isolated, industrial centres.

Rome
With almost 3 million inhabitants, Italy's capital is its most populous city.

In **Belgium**, almost **98 per cent** of the *population* live in **towns and cities**.

In Lapland, near the Arctic Circle in northern Scandinavia, there are few towns and the population density is very low.

ASIA

Mighty continent
Asia extends from the Arctic Ocean in the north to the Indian Ocean in the south, and from the Pacific Ocean in the east, to the Ural Mountains, the Suez Canal, the Bosphorus Strait, and the Caucasus Mountains in the west.

EUROPE

AFRICA

Mediterranean Sea

Russian Federation
Three-quarters of the Russian Federation, commonly known as Russia, lies in Asia, making it the continent's largest country.

Ural'sk

Yekaterin

Istanbul

ANKARA
Black Sea

CYPRUS
NICOSIA
BEIRUT
LEBANON
Aleppo
TURKEY
GEORGIA
ARMENIA
TBILISI

K A Z A K H S T A N

Israel
The State of Israel was established in 1948.

DAMASCUS
JERUSALEM
AMMAN
ISRAEL
SYRIA
Mosul
JORDAN

YEREVAN
AZERBAIJAN
BAKU

AZERB.

Aktau

AST

Kara

BAGHDAD

Caspian Sea

Dasoguz

Kyzylorda

SAUDI ARABIA

IRAQ
Basra

TEHRAN

TURKMENISTAN

UZBEKISTAN

Jedda
Mecca

KUWAIT
KUWAIT

ASHGABAT

Mashhad

TASHKENT

Shymkent

BISHKEK

RIYADH

BAHRAIN
MANAMA
QATAR
DOHA

Shiraz

IRAN

Herat

Samarqand

DUSHANBE

KYRGYZSTAN

UAE
Dubai

Al

SANA

ABU DHABI

MUSCAT

AFGHANISTAN

KABUL
TAJIKISTAN

Quetta

ISLAMABAD

(claimed by Ind

YEMEN

OMAN

Gulf of Oman

Peshawar

(line of control)

(administe
China, clai
by India)

Aden

Gulf of Aden

PAKISTAN
Lahore

Karachi

Hyderabad

NEW DELHI

Arabian Sea

Ahmadabad

Jaipur

Kanpur

NEPAL

KATHMANDU

Bhopal

Patna

THIM

INDIA

BH

Mumbai
(Bombay)

Nagpur

Kolkata
(Calcutta)

BANGLA

Hyderabad

MYAN
(BUR

Bangalore

Chennai
(Madras)

Kochi

India
With a population of 1.27 billion, India is the world's largest democracy.

Bay of Bengal

(Ra

MALE'

COLOMBO
SRI LANKA
SRI JAYEWARDENAPURA KOTTE

MALDIVES

*Andam
Sea*

Nicobar Islands
(to India)

I N D I A N

O C E A N

Med

FAST FACTS

Total land area:
43,608,000 sq km
(16,837,143 sq miles)

Total population:
4.4 billion

Number of countries: 49

Largest country:
Russian Federation
– 17,098,242 sq km
(6,601,668 sq miles)

Smallest country:
Maldives – 298 sq km
(115 sq miles)

Largest country population:
China – 1.37 billion

Streets packed with people are a common sight in China's cities.

Countries and borders

The vast continent of Asia includes two giant nations – China and India, each with a population of more than a billion people and with rapidly growing economies. To the north is the world's biggest country by area – the Russian Federation. To the west lie the countries of the Middle East, today the centre of the Islamic world.

Indonesia
The world's largest island nation, Indonesia is made up of more than 13,000 islands.

ASIA IS THE ONLY CONTINENT IN THE WORLD THAT

ARCTIC OCEAN

NORTH AMERICA

Kara Sea

Laptev Sea

East Siberian Sea

Noril'sk

Anadyr'

Bering Sea

RUSSIAN FEDERATION

Novosibirsk

Yakutsk

Magadan

Petropavlosk-Kamchatskiy

Sea of Okhotsk

Irkutsk

ey

Khabarovsk

Sea of Japan (East Sea)

Sapporo

ÜRümqi

ULAN BATOR

MONGOLIA

Harbin

Vladivostok

NORTH KOREA

Sendai

aimed by China)

CHINA

Lanzhou

BEIJING

Dalian

PYONGYANG

SOUTH KOREA

SEJONG CITY

Kyoto

TOKYO

Tianjin

SEOUL

Xi'an

Qingdao

Busan

Hiroshima

Osaka

Yellow Sea

Fukuoka

JAPAN

Chengdu

Wuhan

Shanghai

East China Sea

Japan
Japan is a major industrial power and has the world's fourth-largest economy.

Kunming

Guiyang

Fuzhou

alay

AY PYI TAW

Guangzhou

Hong Kong

TAIPEI

Gaoxiong

HANOI

Chiang Mai

VIENTIANE

Da Nang

TAIWAN

N

China
Relatively closed to the outside world until the 1970s, China now plays a major role on the world's political stage.

PHILIPPINES

MANILA

Philippine Sea

THAILAND

BANGKOK

CAMBODIA

PHNOM PENH

Ho Chi Minh City

Gulf of Thailand

KEY

⬤ Capital city

⬤ Major city

LA PUR

TRAJAYA

INGAPORE

SINGAPORE

South China Sea

BANDAR SERI BEGAWAN

BRUNEI

Cebu

Davao

PACIFIC

MALAYSIA

OCEAN

Dividing line
The western half of the island of New Guinea lies in Asia; the eastern half is in Australasia and Oceania.

ng

N

D

O

N

E

JAKARTA

Java Sea

S

I

A

Bandung

Makassar

Jayapura

Semarang

Surabaya

Flores Sea

DILI

EAST TIMOR

Arafura Sea

Timor Sea

SHARES BORDERS WITH THREE OTHER CONTINENTS.

EUROPE

Dead Sea
A salt lake bordering Israel, the West Bank, and Jordan. At 392 m (1,286 ft) below sea level, it is the lowest land point on Earth's surface.

West Siberian Plain
One of the largest plains in the world, it is a vast system of marshes.

Mediterranean Sea

Black Sea

Anatolia

Caucasus

Ural Mo...

We...

Siber...

Pla...

Aral Sea

③ *Caspian Sea*

Kirghiz Stepp...

Dead Sea
-392 m /
-1,286 ft

Syrian Desert

Euphrates

Tigris

Kara Kum

Amu Darya

Syr Darya

Lake Balk...

AFRICA

Red Sea

Arabian Peninsula

Persian Gulf

Zagros Mountains

Iranian Plateau

Hindu Kush

K2
8,611 m /
28,251 ft

Tien Shan

Takla Makan Desert

Kunlun Mount...

Ar Rub' al Khálí (Empty Quarter)

Gulf of Oman

Indus

Thar Desert

Mount Everest
8,848 m /
29,029 ft

H i m a l a...

Plat...
of T...

Gulf of Aden   Socotra

Arabian Sea

Ganges

Brahm...

①

FAST FACTS

① **Highest point:**
Mount Everest, Nepal/Tibet, China – 8,848 m (29,029 ft)

④ **Largest island:**
Borneo – 748,168 sq km (288,869 sq miles)

② **Longest river:**
Yangtze, China – 6,380 km (3,964 miles)

③ **Largest lake:**
Caspian Sea – 371,000 sq km (143,243 sq miles)

④ Borneo is the largest island in Asia, and the third-largest island in the world.

Western Ghats

Deccan

Eastern Ghats

Indian Shield
Its collision with the Eurasian Plate has created the Himalayas, the world's highest mountain system.

Bay of Bengal

Andaman Islands

Sri Lanka

Andaman Sea

Nicobar Islands

INDIAN OCEAN

Suma...

Landscape

Asia covers approximately 30 per cent of Earth's land area and makes up the eastern portion of the Eurasian supercontinent (with Europe lying to the west). It is made up of five different landscapes: mountain systems, plateaus, plains, steppes (large areas of unforested grassland), and deserts.

Indonesian islands
Indonesia is the most volcanic country in the world. It is home to 147 volcanoes, 76 of which are active.

ns

Kara Sea

Ob'

Yenisey

Laptev
Sea

Central
Siberian
Plateau

Lena

Siberia

Wrangel
Island

Chukchi
Sea

East Siberian
Sea

NORTH
AMERICA

Bering
Sea

Aldan

Kamchatka

Altai Mountains

Plateau of
Mongolia

Lake
Baikal

Gobi

Amur

Sea of
Okhotsk

Sakhalin

Kurile Islands

Qilian Shan

Yellow River

Khrebet Sikhote-Alin

Hokkaido

Mekong

Salween

Sichuan
Pendi

Great
Plain of
China

Shandong
Peninsula

Sea of
Japan
(East Sea)

Honshu

Yangtze

②

Yellow
Sea

East
China
Sea

Korea Strait

Kyushu

Shikoku

Japan
The country is made
up of 6,852 islands,
of which the largest
is Honshu.

Red River

Xi Jiang

Taiwan Strait

Hainan

Great Plain of China
This relatively flat area of
land is one of the most
densely populated
regions in the world.

Taiwan

Ryukyu Islands

Mekong

PACIFIC

Luzon

Ph

OCEAN

Philippine
Sea

KEY
The colours on the map
represent the height of
the land in relation to
sea level.

f Thailand

South
China
Sea

Palawan

Natuna
Islands

eater

Sunda

④ Borneo

Islands

Celebes
Sea

Mindanao

Halmahera

ELEVATION

Feet	Metres
above 26,247	above 8,000
22,965	7,000
19,685	6,000
16,404	5,000
13,123	4,000
9,842	3,000
6,560	2,000
3,280	1,000
Sea level 0	0 Sea level

Java
Sea

Java

E

Celebes

Flores Sea

Lesser

Sunda Islands

Banda
Sea

Flores

Timor

Moluccas

Seram

Timor Sea

Arafura
Sea

New Guinea

N

Fascinating facts

Number of time zones

16

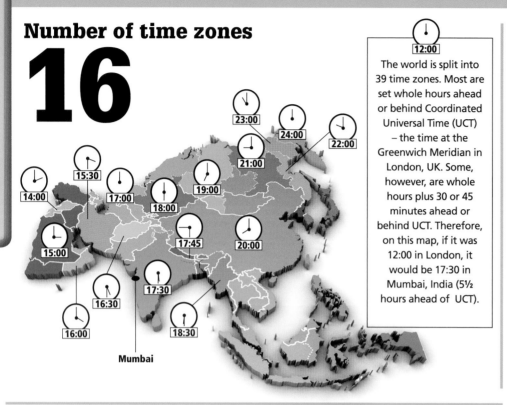

12:00

The world is split into 39 time zones. Most are set whole hours ahead or behind Coordinated Universal Time (UCT) – the time at the Greenwich Meridian in London, UK. Some, however, are whole hours plus 30 or 45 minutes ahead or behind UCT. Therefore, on this map, if it was 12:00 in London, it would be 17:30 in Mumbai, India (5½ hours ahead of UCT).

23:00 · 24:00 · 22:00 · 21:00 · 15:30 · 19:00 · 14:00 · 17:00 · 18:00 · 15:00 · 17:45 · 20:00 · 16:30 · 17:30 · 16:00 · 18:30

Mumbai

13 Landlocked countries

Afghanistan ▪ Armenia ▪ Azerbaijan ▪ Belarus ▪ Bhutan ▪ Kazakhstan ▪ Kyrgyzstan ▪ Laos ▪ Mongolia ▪ Nepal ▪ Tajikistan ▪ Turkmenistan ▪ Uzbekistan

Fastest train
Shanghai Maglev Train, China – **430 km/h (267.2 mph)**

Longest tunnels

 Railway tunnel
Seikan Tunnel, Tsugaru Strait, Japan – 53.85 km (33.5 miles)

 Metro line
Guangzhou Metro Line 3, Guangzhou, China – 60.4 km (37.5 miles)

 Road tunnel
Xishan Tunnel, Shanxi, China – 13.65 km (8.5 miles)

Tallest buildings

Burj Khalifa Dubai, UAE 828 m (2,715 ft)

Shanghai Tower Shanghai, China 632 m (2,073 ft)

Makkah Royal Clock Tower Mecca, Saudi Arabia 601 m (1,971 ft)

Taipei 101 Taipei, Taiwan 509 m (1,670 ft)

Shanghai World Finance Centre Shanghai, China 492 m (1,614 ft)

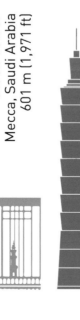
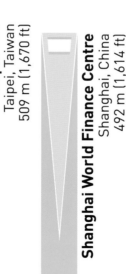

 Longest coastline Indonesia – **54,716 km (33,999 miles)**

✈ **Busiest airport** Beijing International Airport, China – **90.203 million passengers per year**

Biggest glacier
Fedchenko Glacier, Tajikistan – 77 km (48 miles) long
The Fedchenko Glacier is the longest glacier in the world outside of the polar regions

WATERFALLS

Highest:
Hannoki Falls, Toyama, Japan – 500 m (1,640 ft)

Largest (by volume):
Chutes de Khone, Laos – 11,610 m³ (410,000 ft³) of water per second

Deepest lake

Lake Baikal, Russian Federation –
1,642 m (5,387 ft)

Lake Baikal is the deepest lake in the world

Most active volcano

Mount Merapi, Indonesia

Asia's extreme points

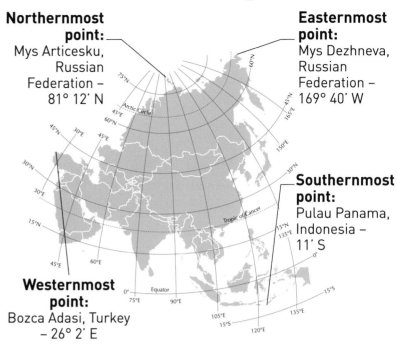

Northernmost point:
Mys Articesku, Russian Federation – 81° 12' N

Easternmost point:
Mys Dezhneva, Russian Federation – 169° 40' W

Southernmost point:
Pulau Panama, Indonesia – 11' S

Westernmost point:
Bozca Adasi, Turkey – 26° 2' E

Highest mountains

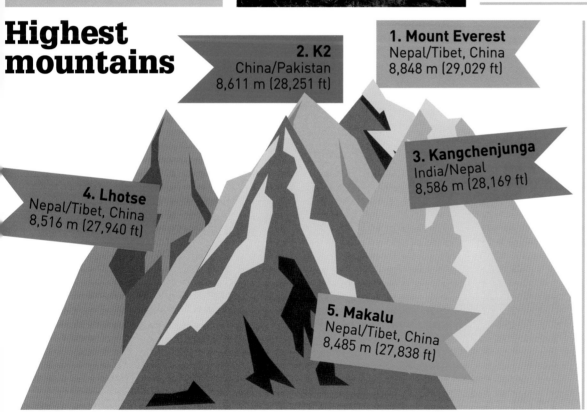

1. Mount Everest
Nepal/Tibet, China
8,848 m (29,029 ft)

2. K2
China/Pakistan
8,611 m (28,251 ft)

3. Kangchenjunga
India/Nepal
8,586 m (28,169 ft)

4. Lhotse
Nepal/Tibet, China
8,516 m (27,940 ft)

5. Makalu
Nepal/Tibet, China
8,485 m (27,838 ft)

Most visited cities (Visitors per year)

Bangkok, Thailand
18.24 million

Singapore
11.88 million

Kuala Lumpur, Malaysia
11.12 million

Seoul, South Korea
10.35 million

Hong Kong
8.66 million

Highest bridge

Duge Beipan River Bridge, Liupanshui, Guizhou, China – **535 m (1,854 ft)**

The world's three highest bridges are all in Asia:
• Duge Beipan River Bridge – 565 m (1,854 ft)
• Sidu River Bridge – 496 m (1,627 ft)
• Puli Bridge– 485 m (1,591 ft)

Longest bridge Danyang–Kunshan Grand Bridge (Beijing–Shanghai high-speed railway) – **164.8 km (102.4 miles)**

This is the longest bridge of any type in the world

Bahrain
Bahrain has a population of 1.3 million, but projections suggest that figure will double in 10 years – the fastest growth rate of any Asian country.

Turkey
Turkey is the most populous country in the Middle East, with a population of 80.3 million.

Bangladesh
Of all the countries in the world with a population of over 100 million, Bangladesh has the highest population density – 1,138 people per sq km (2,948 per sq mile).

India
India has the world's second-largest population (1.27 billion), but is expected to be the world's most-populous country by 2028.

Asia's largest cities

The list below is based on the number of people living inside a city's boundaries.

1. **Shanghai, China –** 24.3 million
2. **Karachi, Pakistan –** 23.5 million
3. **Beijing, China –** 21.5 million
4. **Delhi, India –** 16.4 million
5. **Tianjin, China –** 15.2 million
6. **Tokyo, Japan –** 13.5 million
7. **Guangzhou, China –** 13.1 million
8. **Mumbai, India –** 12.4 million
9. **Shenzhen, China –** 10.5 million
10. **Jakarta, Indonesia –** 10.1 million

The bright lights and busy streets of Tokyo – Japan's largest city.

Population

Asia contains some of the most populous regions on Earth. The plains of eastern China, the Ganges-Brahmaputra rivers in India, Japan, and the Indonesian island of Jakarta all have very high population densities. By contrast, Siberia and the Plateau of Tibet are virtually uninhabited.

KEY
The colours represent the number of people living per square kilometre/square mile.

POPULATION DENSITY

people per sq mile	people per sq km
above 2,600	above 1,000
1,950	750
1,300	500
650	250
260	100
130	50

OVER HALF OF ASIA'S POPULATION OF 4.5 BILLION LIVES IN

Mongolia
The least densely populated country in Asia, with an average of 2 inhabitants per sq km (4 people per sq mile).

Almost **two-thirds** of the world's population live **in Asia**.

China
With a population of 1.37 billion people, China is home to approximately one-fifth of the world's population.

Shanghai
With a population of 24.3 million, Shanghai, China, located on the country's east coast, is the most populous city in the world.

Shanghai's Pudong district is on the banks of the Huangpu River.

Java
The Indonesian island is the world's most populous island – 139.4 million people live there.

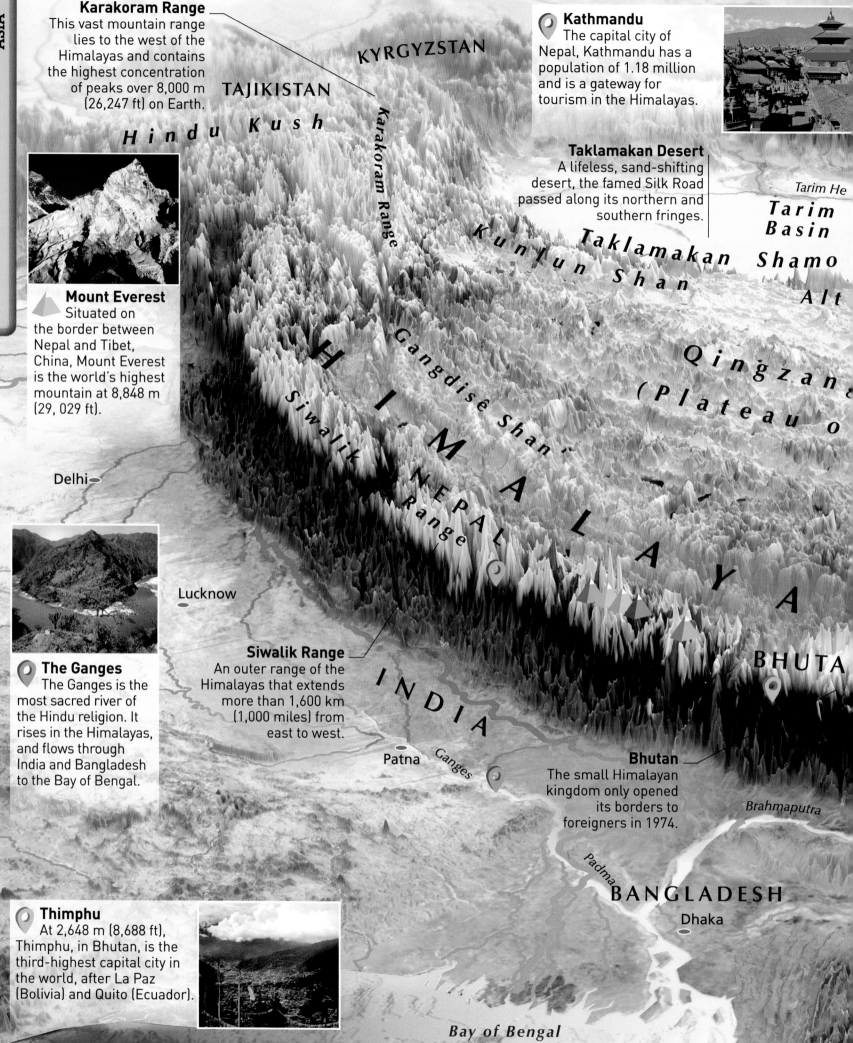

Karakoram Range
This vast mountain range lies to the west of the Himalayas and contains the highest concentration of peaks over 8,000 m (26,247 ft) on Earth.

KYRGYZSTAN

TAJIKISTAN

Hindu Kush

Kathmandu
The capital city of Nepal, Kathmandu has a population of 1.18 million and is a gateway for tourism in the Himalayas.

Taklamakan Desert
A lifeless, sand-shifting desert, the famed Silk Road passed along its northern and southern fringes.

Tarim He

Tarim Basin

Taklamakan Shamo

Alt

Karakoram Range

Kunlun Shan

Mount Everest
Situated on the border between Nepal and Tibet, China, Mount Everest is the world's highest mountain at 8,848 m (29, 029 ft).

Qingzan

(Plateau o

Gangdisê Shan

Siwalik

H I M A L A Y A

NEPAL Range

Delhi

BHUTA

Lucknow

The Ganges
The Ganges is the most sacred river of the Hindu religion. It rises in the Himalayas, and flows through India and Bangladesh to the Bay of Bengal.

Siwalik Range
An outer range of the Himalayas that extends more than 1,600 km (1,000 miles) from east to west.

I N D I A

Patna

Ganges

Bhutan
The small Himalayan kingdom only opened its borders to foreigners in 1974.

Brahmaputra

Thimphu
At 2,648 m (8,688 ft), Thimphu, in Bhutan, is the third-highest capital city in the world, after La Paz (Bolivia) and Quito (Ecuador).

Padma

BANGLADESH

Dhaka

Bay of Bengal

THE HIMALAYAS ARE STILL RISING AT A RATE OF 4 MM (0.25 IN) PER

The Himalayas

The Himalayas is the world's highest mountain range. It runs in an arc 2,400 km (1,500 miles) long, spread across five countries: Pakistan, India, Nepal, Bhutan, and China. It is also the source of some of the region's major rivers, including the mighty Ganges and Brahmaputra rivers.

Plateau of Tibet
The world's largest and highest plateau, it contains the largest amount of ice found outside the poles.

Qilian Shan

Qaidam Pendi

an

aoyuan

ibet)

g Co

C H I N A

Lha

Nyainqentanglha Shan

Tsangpo Gorge
With an average depth of 5,000 m (16,400 ft), Tsangpo Gorge, in Tibet, China, is the deepest canyon in the world.

HIGHEST PEAKS
The Himalayas is home to more than 110 mountains over 7,300 m (24,000 ft). The top five are:

Mount Everest 8,848 m (29,029 ft)

Kangchenjunga 8,586 m (28,169 ft)

Lhotse 8,516 m (27,940 ft)

Makalu 8,462 m (27,765 ft)

Cho Oyu 8,201 m (26,905 ft)

Brahmaputra River
One of Asia's major rivers, it cuts through China, Bhutan, India, and Bangladesh before flowing into the Bay of Bengal.

Makkah Royal Clock Tower
The tower contains the world's largest clock face.

Dome of the Rock
The world's oldest-standing Islamic monument, it dates to the seventh century CE.

Fortress of Nisa
The fortress forms part of an ancient city that was totally destroyed by an earthquake in the first decade BCE.

Dome of the Rock, *Jerusalem, Israel*

Ziggurat of Ur, *Nasiriyah, Iraq*

Makkah Royal Clock Tower, *Mecca, Saudi Arabia*

Fortress of Nisa, *Turkmenistan*

Citadel of Herat, *Afghanistan*

Mausoleum of Kho Ahmed Yasui, *Turkestan, Kazakh*

Shah-i-Zinda Mausoleum *Samarkand, Uzbekist*

Great Mosque of Sana'a, *Yemen*

Persepolis, *Marvdasht, Iran*

Burj Khalifa, *Dubai, UAE*

Badshahi Mosque, *Lahore, Pakistan*

Citadel of Herat
Dates back to 330 BCE, when Alexander the Great arrived in Herat with his army.

Gateway of India, *Mumbai, India*

Taj Mahal, *Agra, India*

Po Pal Lh Tibet, C

● Burj Khalifa

Standing at 828 m (2,715 ft), the Burj Khalifa in Dubai, UAE, is the tallest manmade structure in the world. Completed in 2009, it has 163 floors (including the world's highest observation deck on the 148th floor), 57 elevators, and eight escalators.

Meenakshi Amman Temple, *Madurai, India*

Taj Mahal
The white-marble mausoleum (a building that covers a burial chamber) attracts 8 million visitors a year.

Bagar *Myanma*

Meenakshi Amman Temple
This Hindu temple lies at the heart of the ancient Indian city of Madurai.

Petronas Towers
At 452 m (1,483 ft), they are the world's tallest twin towers.

Famous landmarks

Asia is a continent of huge contrasts. It was the birthplace of some of the earliest human civilizations, has been a hub for many of the world's great religions, such as Islam, Hinduism, and Buddhism, and, today, is the site of some of the world's most amazing modern architecture.

KEY
○ Landmark location

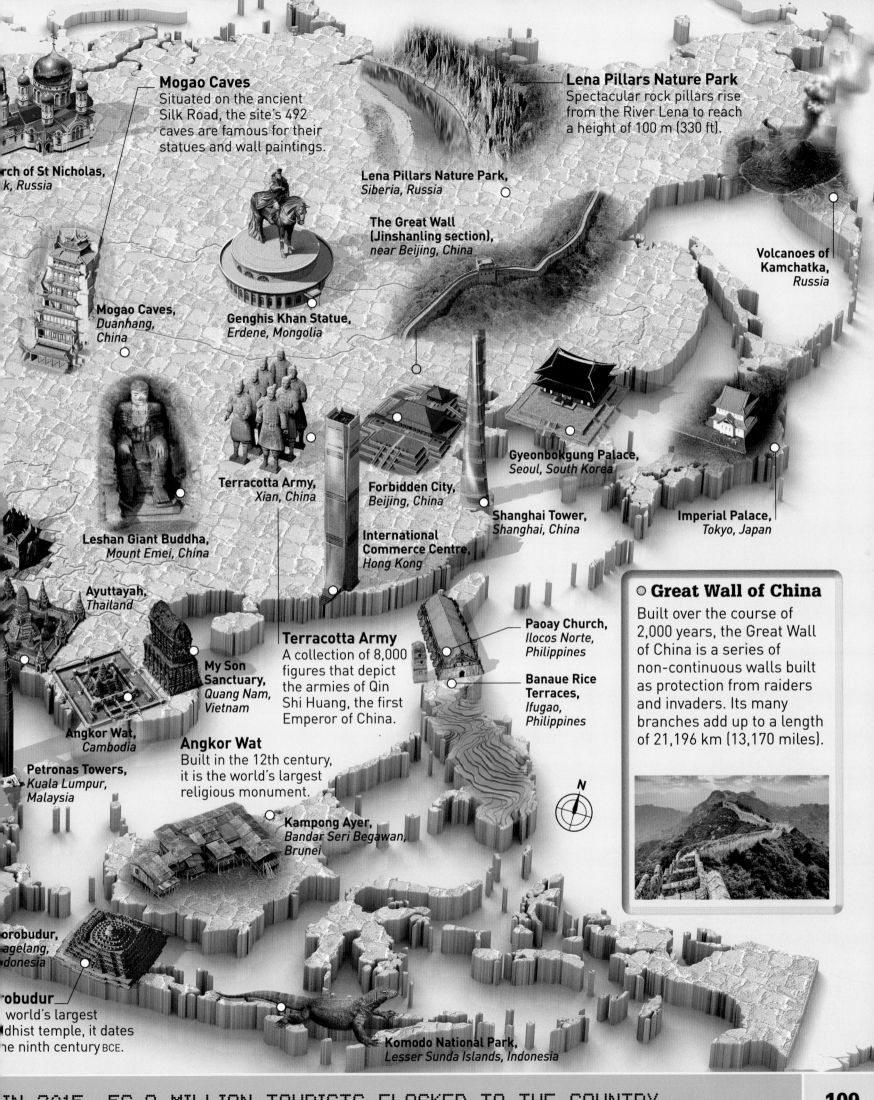

Mogao Caves
Situated on the ancient Silk Road, the site's 492 caves are famous for their statues and wall paintings.

Lena Pillars Nature Park
Spectacular rock pillars rise from the River Lena to reach a height of 100 m (330 ft).

rch of St Nicholas,
k, Russia

Lena Pillars Nature Park,
Siberia, Russia

The Great Wall
(Jinshanling section),
near Beijing, China

Volcanoes of
Kamchatka,
Russia

Mogao Caves,
*Duanhang,
China*

Genghis Khan Statue,
Erdene, Mongolia

Gyeonbokgung Palace,
Seoul, South Korea

Imperial Palace,
Tokyo, Japan

Terracotta Army,
Xian, China

Forbidden City,
Beijing, China

Shanghai Tower,
Shanghai, China

Leshan Giant Buddha,
Mount Emei, China

International
Commerce Centre,
Hong Kong

○ Great Wall of China
Built over the course of 2,000 years, the Great Wall of China is a series of non-continuous walls built as protection from raiders and invaders. Its many branches add up to a length of 21,196 km (13,170 miles).

Ayuttayah,
Thailand

Terracotta Army
A collection of 8,000 figures that depict the armies of Qin Shi Huang, the first Emperor of China.

Paoay Church,
*Ilocos Norte,
Philippines*

My Son
Sanctuary,
*Quang Nam,
Vietnam*

Banaue Rice
Terraces,
*Ifugao,
Philippines*

Angkor Wat,
Cambodia

Angkor Wat
Built in the 12th century, it is the world's largest religious monument.

Petronas Towers,
*Kuala Lumpur,
Malaysia*

Kampong Ayer,
*Bandar Seri Begawan,
Brunei*

N

orobudur,
agelang,
donesia

robudur
world's largest
dhist temple, it dates
he ninth century BCE.

Komodo National Park,
Lesser Sunda Islands, Indonesia

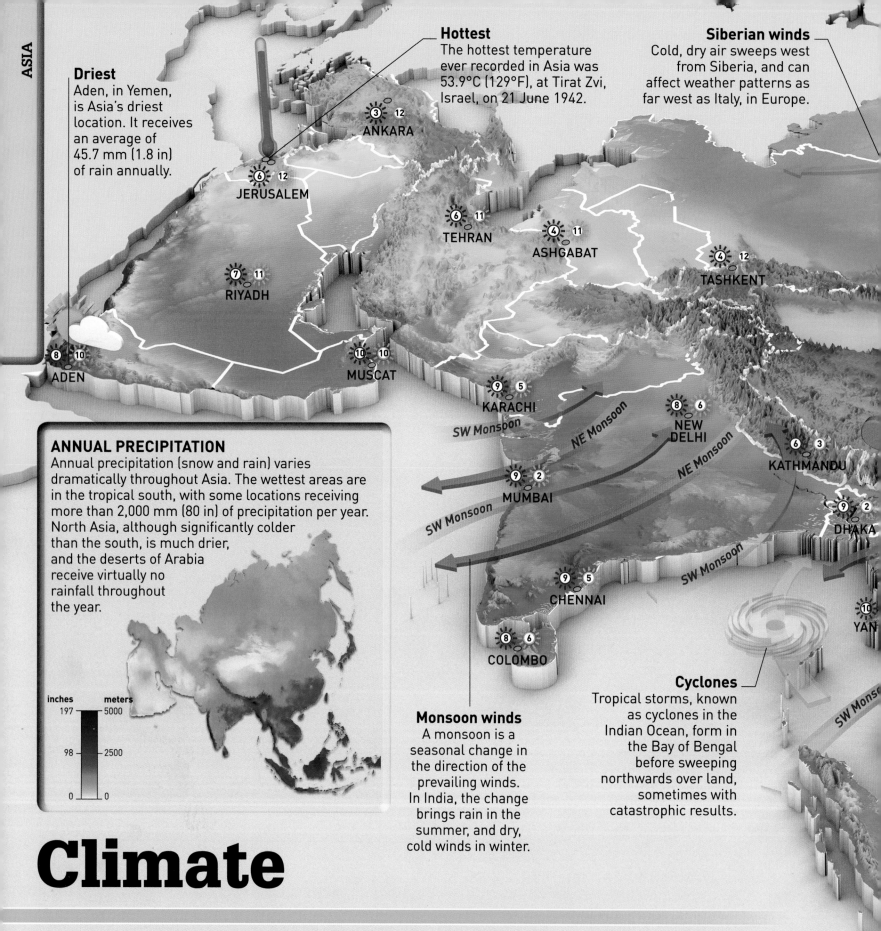

Driest
Aden, in Yemen, is Asia's driest location. It receives an average of 45.7 mm (1.8 in) of rain annually.

Hottest
The hottest temperature ever recorded in Asia was 53.9°C (129°F), at Tirat Zvi, Israel, on 21 June 1942.

Siberian winds
Cold, dry air sweeps west from Siberia, and can affect weather patterns as far west as Italy, in Europe.

ANKARA 3 · 12
JERUSALEM 6 · 12
TEHRAN 6 · 11
ASHGABAT 4 · 11
TASHKENT 4 · 12
RIYADH 7 · 11
ADEN 8 · 10
MUSCAT 10 · 10
KARACHI 9 · 5
NEW DELHI 8 · 6
KATHMANDU 6 · 3
MUMBAI 9 · 2
DHAKA 9 · 2
CHENNAI 9 · 5
COLOMBO 8 · 6
YAN 10

SW Monsoon
NE Monsoon
NE Monsoon
SW Monsoon
SW Monsoon
SW Monsoon
SW Monso

ANNUAL PRECIPITATION
Annual precipitation (snow and rain) varies dramatically throughout Asia. The wettest areas are in the tropical south, with some locations receiving more than 2,000 mm (80 in) of precipitation per year. North Asia, although significantly colder than the south, is much drier, and the deserts of Arabia receive virtually no rainfall throughout the year.

inches	meters
197	5000
98	2500
0	0

Monsoon winds
A monsoon is a seasonal change in the direction of the prevailing winds. In India, the change brings rain in the summer, and dry, cold winds in winter.

Cyclones
Tropical storms, known as cyclones in the Indian Ocean, form in the Bay of Bengal before sweeping northwards over land, sometimes with catastrophic results.

Climate

Because of its enormous size, the climate in Asia varies dramatically, from the polar cold of the north, to the dry, desert environments of the southwest and centre, and the hot, humid conditions of the tropical south. The continent is home to some of the coldest, hottest, driest, and wettest places on Earth.

LIFE IN ASIA IS CRITICALLY DEPENDENT ON MONSOON RAINS. A WEAK

Coldest
On 5 and 7 February 1892, the temperature fell to -67.8°C (-90°F) in Verkhoyansk, Russia – the lowest temperature ever recorded in Asia.

YAKUTSK

ALEKHARD

ANADYR'

PETROPAVLOVSK-KAMCHATSKIY

YENISEYSK

ÜMQI

East Asian monsoon
In East Asia, prevailing winds change direction during the year, bringing a warm, wet summer monsoon and a cold, dry winter monsoon.

Wettest
Meghalaya State in India holds the world record for the average amount of precipitation received annually: 11,872 mm (467.4 in) per year.

BEIJING

SEOUL

TOKYO

CHONGQING

KUNMING

SHANGHAI

HANOI

HONG KONG

NE Monsoon

KOK

PHNOM PENH

Typhoons
Tropical storms are called typhoons in the Pacific Ocean. The storm season typically occurs between May and October.

MANILA

N

KEY
The scale on the right represents average annual temperatures, with dark red being the hottest and dark blue being the coldest.

90°F — 32°C

32°F — 0°C

-20°F — -29°C

AVERAGE HOURS OF SUNSHINE

☼ Jan   ☀ July

⬭ Town/city

🌀 Cyclone/typhoon

➡ Warm winds

➡ Cold winds

➡ Direction of tropical storms

GAPORE

RTA

BANDAR SERI BEGAWAN

DILI

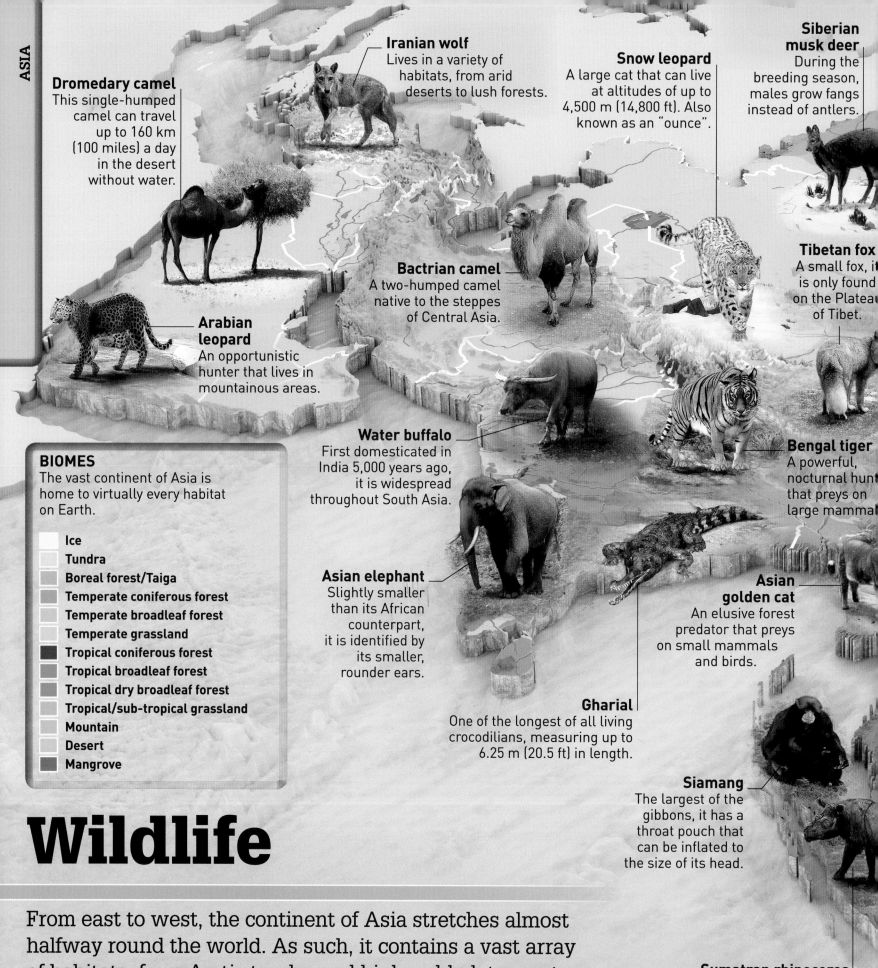

Dromedary camel
This single-humped camel can travel up to 160 km (100 miles) a day in the desert without water.

Iranian wolf
Lives in a variety of habitats, from arid deserts to lush forests.

Snow leopard
A large cat that can live at altitudes of up to 4,500 m (14,800 ft). Also known as an "ounce".

Siberian musk deer
During the breeding season, males grow fangs instead of antlers.

Bactrian camel
A two-humped camel native to the steppes of Central Asia.

Tibetan fox
A small fox, it is only found on the Plateau of Tibet.

Arabian leopard
An opportunistic hunter that lives in mountainous areas.

Water buffalo
First domesticated in India 5,000 years ago, it is widespread throughout South Asia.

Bengal tiger
A powerful, nocturnal hunter that preys on large mammals.

BIOMES
The vast continent of Asia is home to virtually every habitat on Earth.

- Ice
- Tundra
- Boreal forest/Taiga
- Temperate coniferous forest
- Temperate broadleaf forest
- Temperate grassland
- Tropical coniferous forest
- Tropical broadleaf forest
- Tropical dry broadleaf forest
- Tropical/sub-tropical grassland
- Mountain
- Desert
- Mangrove

Asian elephant
Slightly smaller than its African counterpart, it is identified by its smaller, rounder ears.

Asian golden cat
An elusive forest predator that preys on small mammals and birds.

Gharial
One of the longest of all living crocodilians, measuring up to 6.25 m (20.5 ft) in length.

Siamang
The largest of the gibbons, it has a throat pouch that can be inflated to the size of its head.

Wildlife

From east to west, the continent of Asia stretches almost halfway round the world. As such, it contains a vast array of habitats, from Arctic tundra and high, cold plateaus, to barren deserts and damp, lush rainforests. The continent's array of wildlife is as vast and varied as the landscape itself.

Sumatran rhinoceros
The smallest of the rhinoceroses, it is one of the world's most endangered species.

MORE PEOPLE DEPEND ON THE WORLD'S 130 MILLION WATER

Polar bear
The largest land carnivore in the world, it is only found in the Arctic.

Arctic fox
incredibly hardy animal is common throughout the Arctic region.

Baikal seal
Only found in Lake Baikal, Siberia, it is the only true seal that lives exclusively in freshwater.

Steller's sea eagle
Weighing up to 9 kg (20 lb), it is the heaviest eagle in the world.

Giant panda
The rarest member of the bear family, 99 per cent of its diet is bamboo.

Siberian tiger
The largest of the tiger species, it can grow up to 4 m (13 ft) in length.

Japanese macaque
The world's most northern-living primate, it is also known as the "snow monkey".

Yak
Similar to the American bison, it is adapted to living at altitude.

King cobra
Reaching lengths of up to 5.5 m (18 ft), it is the world's longest venomous snake.

Clouded leopard
Named for the distinctive clouded spots on its coat, it is an excellent climber.

Deforestation
The world's third-largest area of tropical rainforest lies in Southeast Asia, but the region is experiencing deforestation at a faster rate than anywhere else on Earth. This has a devastating effect on both the region's wildlife and the global climate.

Dhole
A highly social animal well known for its vocal calls.

Proboscis monkey
Its large, fleshy nose is used to attract mates.

Philippine crocodile
A freshwater crocodile, it has a broad snout and thick, bony plates on its body.

Bornean orangutan
The most intelligent of the primates, its ne translates as man of the forest".

Borneo – 56 per cent of the island's forests were cut down between 1985 and 2001.

Komodo dragon
The world's largest lizard, it can consume 80 per cent of its bodyweight in a single meal.

KEY
Illuminated areas on the map reflect urban, built-up areas and roads, in contrast to rural regions.

■ Rural area

▨ Urban area

Trans-Siberian Railway
Bright lights mark a dotted line across Siberia, showing the route of the Trans-Siberian Railway.

Arabian Peninsula
A large portion of the Arabian Peninsula is an area of desert known as the "Empty Quarter".

Oman
This country had the fastest rate of urbanization in Asia over the past five years (8.54 per cent).

● **Hong Kong**
Hong Kong has a population of 7.35 million, making it the 21st largest city in Asia, but the city is the fourth most densely populated territory on Earth, with a staggering 6,682 inhabitants per sq km (17,294 per sq mile).

Indus Valley
This river valley in northern Pakistan is home to some of the country's largest cities, including Lahore and Islamabad.

India
Home to 1.27 billion people, but only 32.7 per cent of the population live in towns or cities.

Bangkok
Almost one-sixth of Thailand's 68.2 million people live in or around the country's capital, Bangkok.

By night

This satellite image of Asia at night shows how the continent's huge population is concentrated in small pockets of land. India, northern China, the southern Korean peninsula, and Japan are densely populated, whereas Siberia and Central Asia are virtually empty.

Singapore
One of three territories in Asia – along with Hong Kong and Macau – in which the entire population live in an urban environment.

ASIA IS HOME TO THREE OF THE WORLD'S FIVE MOST DENSELY

Tokyo-Yokohama
38 million people live in and around the cities of Tokyo and Yokohama.

North Korea
Almost 61 per cent of North Korea's population of 25.1 million live in an urban environment, but electricity shortages in the country mean few lights shine at night.

Philippines
The National Capital Region of the Philippines, which includes Manila, the country's capital, is home to 12.9 million people.

● **Sri Lanka**
Only 18.4 per cent of Sri Lanka's 22 million population live in towns and cities – the lowest figure of any Asian country.

AUSTRALASIA & OCEANIA

Australasia & Oceania from space
Vast deserts dominate the interior of Australia, contrasting with the fertile southeast. To the north, dense forest covers much of New Guinea, while in the far south, the snowy peaks of New Zealand's mountains stand out clearly.

PACIFIC OCEAN

KEY
- ● Capital city
- ● Major city

Philippine Sea

Northern Mariana Islands (to US)

HAGÅTÑA

Guam (to US)

Wake Island (to US)

MARSHALL ISLANDS

Marshall Islands
Conquered during World War Two, these islands belonged to the United States until 1986.

MAJURO

MELEKEOK

PALAU

PALIKIR

M I C R O N E S I A

TA

K

● NAURU

Bismarck Sea

HONIARA

SOLOMON ISLANDS

PAPUA NEW GUINEA

Solomon Sea

PORT MORESBY

A S I A

Arafura Sea

Coral Sea

VANUATU

PORT

New Caledonia
One of the three groups of islands in the Pacific Ocean that are controlled by France. The others are French Polynesia and Wallis and Futuna.

NO

New Caled (to France)

Gulf of Carpentaria

Cairns ●

Joseph Bonaparte Gulf

Darwin ●

Townsville ●

QUEENSLAND

Lord Howe Is (to Australia)

Timor Sea

NORTHERN

TERRITORY

Alice Springs ●

A U S T R A L I A

Brisbane ●

NEW SOUTH WALES

Sydney ●

WESTERN

SOUTH AUSTRALIA

CANBERRA ●

AUSTRALIAN CAPITAL TERRITORY

AUSTRALIA

Adelaide ●

VICTORIA

Melbourne ●

Tasman Sea

Great Australian Bight

TASMANIA

Hobart ●

Australia
Canberra was chosen to be Australia's capital city in 1908. The country is made up of eight states.

Perth ●

N

THE BRITISH MONARCH, QUEEN ELIZABETH II, IS ALSO

Kiribati

This group of 33 tiny islands is spread over a vast area of the Pacific Ocean. Kiribati was a British colony from 1915 until it gained its independence in 1979.

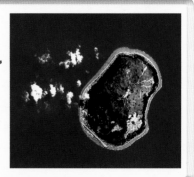

K I R I B A T I

I B A T I

FUNAFITI
ATOLL

TUVALU

Tokelau
(to NZ)

Wallis and
Futuna
(to France)

MATA-
UTU

ÁPIA

SAMOA

PAGO
PAGO

American
Samoa
(to US)

Cook
Islands
(to NZ)

PAPEETE

French
Polynesia
(to France)

SUVA

NUKU'ALOFA

ALOFI

Niue
(to NZ)

AVARUA

FIJI

TONGA

French Polynesia
Tahiti is the largest island in French Polynesia. Many people work in tourism and pearl-farming.

rfolk Island
o Australia)

New Zealand
Most New Zealanders have European ancestors, but about 15 per cent of the population belong to the Maori community. The Maoris arrived in New Zealand in about 1300.

Auckland

NEW
ZEALAND

WELLINGTON

Christchurch

Countries and borders

Australasia is dominated by Australia and New Zealand, two former British colonies that, in recent years, have built new relations with other Pacific nations, such as Japan. Oceania includes the many islands of the Pacific Ocean, whose communities rely increasingly on tourism.

FAST FACTS

Total land area:
8,508,238 sq km
(3,285,049 sq miles)

Total population:
39.7 million

Number of countries: 14

Largest country:
Australia –
7,741,220 sq km
(2,988,901 sq miles)

Smallest country:
Nauru – 21 sq km
(8.1 sq miles)

Largest country population:
Australia – 22.9 million

Australasia and Oceania *(vertical, left margin)*

③ Lake Eyre
With an area of 9,583 sq km (3,700 sq miles), Lake Eyre is the largest lake in Australasia and Oceania. During the dry season, much of the lake evaporates, leaving behind a thick salt crust.

Lake Eyre sometimes turns pink because of a type of algae in the water.

Marshall Islands
A group of 34 scattered atolls (low-lying islands made of coral reefs) in the Pacific Ocean. The average height of each island is only 2 m (6.6 ft) above sea level.

New Guinea
The world's second-largest island after Greenland, New Guinea is dominated by the New Guinea Highlands.

Kimberley Plateau
Rocky gorges and sandstone hills dominate this isolated region of Western Australia.

Great Dividing Range
These mountains divide the fertile coastal plains from the dry interior.

Southern Alps
These young mountains are growing rapidly as the Australian and Pacific plates move towards one another.

Map labels: Micr, Marshall Islands, Ratak Chain, Ralik Chain, Bikini Atoll, Enewetak, Gilbert Is. Tung, Northern Mariana Islands, Mariana Islands, Saipan, Guam, Pohnpei, Kosrae, Chuuk, Tarawa, Yap, Caroline Islands, Melanesi, Nauru, Babeldaob, Mount Wilhelm 4,509 m / 14,793 ft, Bismarck Archipelago, New Ireland, Solomon Islands, Bougainville Island, Tungaru, Santa Cruz Islands, Admiralty Islands, Bismarck Sea, New Britain, Solomon Sea, Espiritu Santo, Philippine Sea, New Guinea, Kikori, Fly, New Georgia Islands, Louisiade Archipelago, Torres Strait, Coral Sea, New Caledon, Arafura Sea, Cape York Peninsula, Great Barrier Reef, Arnhem Land, Gulf of Carpentaria, Joseph Bonaparte Gulf, Barkly Tableland, Lord Howe Island, Timor Sea, Kimberley Plateau, Cape Byron, Tanami Desert, Macdonnell Ranges, Great Sandy Desert, Simpson Desert, Barwon, Uluru (Ayers Rock) 867 m / 2,844 ft, Lake Eyre North ③, Darling, Lachlan, Fortescue, Gibson Desert, Great Victoria Desert, Lake Torrens, Flinders Ranges, Grey Range, Murray ②, Australian Alps, Mount Kosciuszko 2,228 m / 7,310 ft, Tasman Sea, Ashburton, Murchison, Lake Everard, Lake Gairdner, Nullarbor Plain, Great Australian Bight, Kangaroo Island, King Island, Furneaux Group, Tasmania, Darling Range, N

ASIA

Micronesia
Micronesia is a state
of more than 600
islands, many of
which are atolls.

Teraina
Tabuarean
Kiritimati

Line Islands

Malden Island

Kanton

Starbuck Island

Marquesas
Islands

Phoenix Islands

Penrhyn

Millennium
Island

Mururoa

Tokelau

Northern Cook Islands

Manihiki

Vostok
Island

Flint Island

Nuku
Hiva

Tuvalu

American
Samoa

Samoa

Upolu

Tutuila

Cook
Islands

Hiva Oa

Rangiroa

Rotuma

Wallis and
Futuna

Savai'i

Bora-Bora

Society Islands

Tuamotu Islands

Vanua
Levu

Raiatea

Tahiti

Hao

Southern Cook Islands

Viti
Levu

Fiji

Niue

Lau
Group

ngo
na

Tonga

Rarotonga

Mauke

*French
Polynesia*

Îles Australes

Îles
Gambier

Fiji
A volcanic archipelago
consisting of two main
islands and 880
smaller islands.

P   o   l   y   n

Rapa

Norfolk
sland

P   O   l   y

North Island
Most of New
Zealand's active
volcanoes are found
on the North Island.

PACIFIC
OCEAN

Bay of
Plenty

**New
Zealand**

North
Island

Cook Strait

raki (Mt Cook)
3,724 m /
12,218 ft

Southern Alps

Landscape

South
Island

Stewart
Island

Auckland
Islands

The Australian landscape is dominated by ancient
mountain ranges and unusual rock formations.
New Zealand is a land of earthquakes, volcanoes,
and geysers. Oceania is made up of approximately
10,000 islands in the Pacific Ocean.

KEY
The colours on the
map represent the
height of the land in
relation to sea level.

ELEVATION

Feet	Metres
above 26,247	above 8,000
22,965	7,000
19,685	6,000
16,404	5,000
13,123	4,000
9,842	3,000
6,560	2,000
3,280	1,000
Sea level 0	0 Sea level

Fascinating facts

COUNTRY WITH THE MOST NEIGHBOURS

Papua New Guinea

1 – Indonesia

LONGEST TUNNELS

Railway tunnel
Kaimai Tunnel, North Island, New Zealand – 8.85 km (5.5 miles)

Road tunnel
Airport Link, Brisbane, Australia – 6.7 km (4.16 miles)

Number of time zones

11

The world is split into 39 time zones. Most are set whole hours ahead or behind Coordinated Universal Time (UCT) – the time at the Greenwich Meridian in London, UK. Some, however, are whole hours plus 30 or 45 minutes ahead or behind UCT. Therefore, on this map, if it was 12:00 in London, it would be 22:00 in Sydney, Australia (10 hours ahead of UCT).

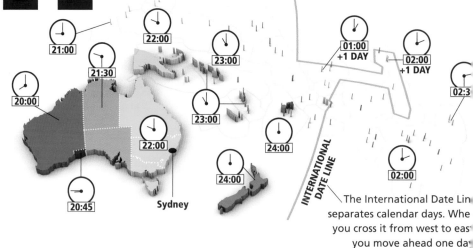

The International Date Line separates calendar days. When you cross it from west to east, you move ahead one day.

Longest coastline
Australia – **25,760 km (16,006.5 miles)**

Busiest port
Port Hedland, Western Australia – **488,000 kilotons of cargo per year,** making it the eighth-busiest port in the world

Fastest train
Tilt Train, Australia – **210 km/h (130.5 mph)**

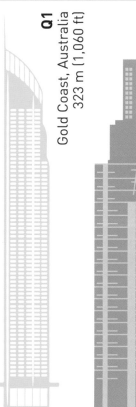

Q1
Gold Coast, Australia
323 m (1,060 ft)

Tallest buildings

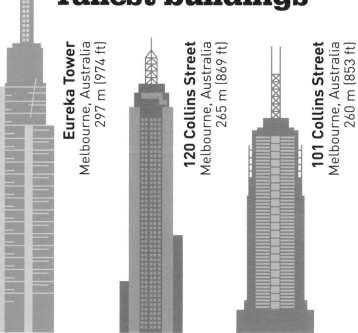

Eureka Tower
Melbourne, Australia
297 m (974 ft)

120 Collins Street
Melbourne, Australia
265 m (869 ft)

101 Collins Street
Melbourne, Australia
260 m (853 ft)

Prima Pearl
Melbourne, Australia

Busiest airport Sydney Airport, Sydney, Australia – **39.7 million passengers per year**

BRIDGES

Longest bridge: Macleay River Bridge, Australia – **3.2 km (2 miles)**

○ **Highest bridge:** Mohaka Viaduct, Raupunga, New Zealand – **95 m (312 ft)**

WATERFALLS

Highest: **Browne Falls, New Zealand** – 836 m (2,744 ft)

Largest (by volume): **Huka Falls, Taupo, New Zealand** – 220 m³ (7,769 ft³) of water per second

LAKES

Largest lake: Lake Eyre, Australia – **9,583 sq km (3,700 sq miles)**

○ **Deepest lake:** Lake Hauroko, New Zealand – **462 m (1,516 ft)**

Most visited cities (Visitors per year)

Sydney, Australia
2.853 million

Melbourne, Australia
2.166 million

Auckland, NZ
1.965 million

Christchurch, NZ
1.732 million

Brisbane, Australia
1.066 million

Highest mountains

2. Mount Giluwe
Papua New Guinea
4,368 m (14,331 ft)

1. Mount Wilhelm
Papua New Guinea
4,509 m (14,793 ft)

3. Mount Herbert
Papua New Guinea
4,267 m (13,999 ft)

4. Mount Bangeta
Papua New Guinea
4,121 m (13,520 ft)

5. Mount Victoria
Papua New Guinea
4,072 m (13,360 ft)

HIGHEST VOLCANO

Mount Giluwe, Papua New Guinea – **4,368 m (14,331 ft)**

Australasia and Oceania's extreme points

Northernmost point: Eastern Island, Midway Islands 28° 15′ N

Westernmost point: Cape Inscription, Australia 112° 57′ E

Easternmost point: Ducie Island 124° 47′ W

Southernmost point: Macquarie Island, NZ 54° 30′ S

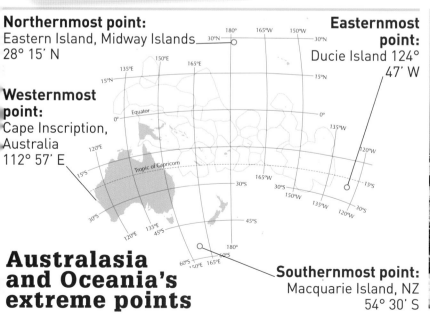

BIGGEST GLACIER

Tasman Glacier, New Zealand – **27 km (17 miles) long, with an area of 101 sq km (39 sq miles)**

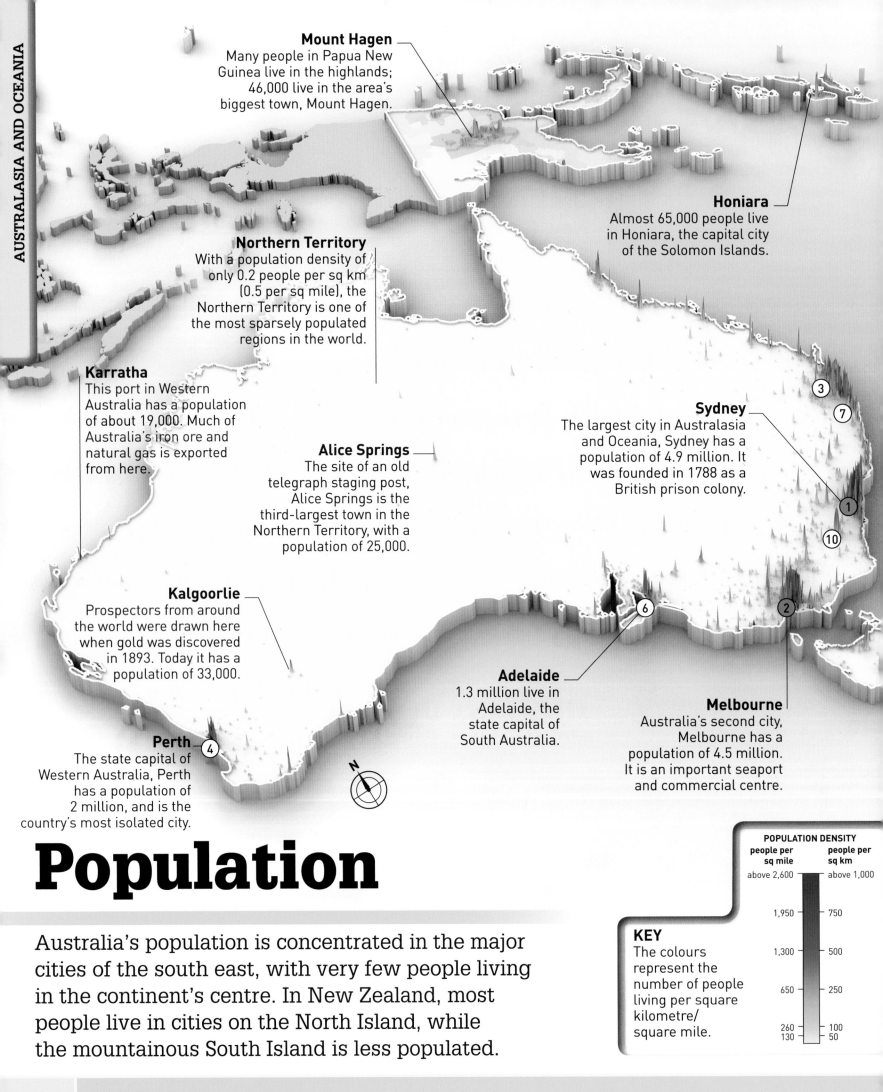

Mount Hagen
Many people in Papua New Guinea live in the highlands; 46,000 live in the area's biggest town, Mount Hagen.

Honiara
Almost 65,000 people live in Honiara, the capital city of the Solomon Islands.

Northern Territory
With a population density of only 0.2 people per sq km (0.5 per sq mile), the Northern Territory is one of the most sparsely populated regions in the world.

Karratha
This port in Western Australia has a population of about 19,000. Much of Australia's iron ore and natural gas is exported from here.

Sydney
The largest city in Australasia and Oceania, Sydney has a population of 4.9 million. It was founded in 1788 as a British prison colony.

Alice Springs
The site of an old telegraph staging post, Alice Springs is the third-largest town in the Northern Territory, with a population of 25,000.

Kalgoorlie
Prospectors from around the world were drawn here when gold was discovered in 1893. Today it has a population of 33,000.

Adelaide
1.3 million live in Adelaide, the state capital of South Australia.

Melbourne
Australia's second city, Melbourne has a population of 4.5 million. It is an important seaport and commercial centre.

Perth
The state capital of Western Australia, Perth has a population of 2 million, and is the country's most isolated city.

Population

Australia's population is concentrated in the major cities of the south east, with very few people living in the continent's centre. In New Zealand, most people live in cities on the North Island, while the mountainous South Island is less populated.

POPULATION DENSITY

people per sq mile	people per sq km
above 2,600	above 1,000
1,950	750
1,300	500
650	250
260	100
130	50

KEY The colours represent the number of people living per square kilometre/square mile.

Fiji
Fiji has a population of 915,303. Its largest town is Nasinu, which is home to 87,000 people.

Auckland
New Zealand's largest city, Auckland is home to one-third of the country's population.

Christchurch
380,000 people live in Christchurch, the largest city in New Zealand's South Island.

Wellington
New Zealand's capital, Wellington has a population of 400,000 and is the country's second-largest city.

Australasia and Oceania's largest cities

The list below is based on the number of people living inside a city's boundaries.

① **Sydney, Australia –** 4.9 million

② **Melbourne, Australia –** 4.5 million

③ **Brisbane, Australia –** 2.3 million

④ **Perth, Australia –** 2 million

⑤ **Auckland, New Zealand –** 1.4 million

⑥ **Adelaide, Australia –** 1.3 million

⑦ **Gold Coast, Australia –** 530,000

⑧ **Wellington, New Zealand –** 400,000

⑨ **Christchurch, New Zealand –** 389,000

⑩ **Canberra, Australia –** 380,000

Melbourne is the capital city of the Australian state of Victoria.

Almost *one in three* Australians were born **outside** the country.

BY NIGHT
The brightly lit cities of southeastern Australia shine brightly, and Sydney, Melbourne, and Brisbane are easy to spot. In contrast, the country's interior is shrouded in darkness. Auckland and Wellington are two of the bright points on New Zealand's North Island, with only Christchurch standing out on South Island.

KEY

■ Rural area

▨ Urban area

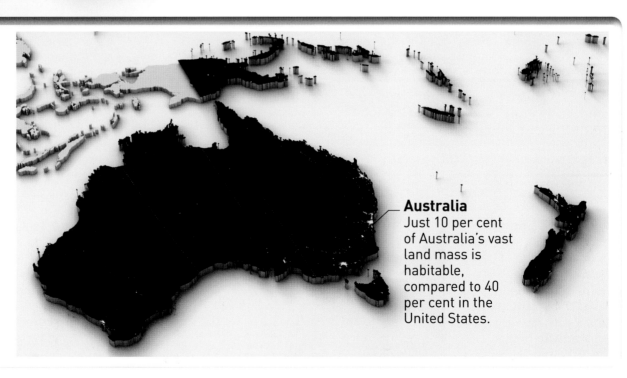

Australia
Just 10 per cent of Australia's vast land mass is habitable, compared to 40 per cent in the United States.

New Zealand

Almost one-third of New Zealand has been set aside as protected national park. Among its incredible range of landscapes are the towering peaks of the Southern Alps, and the geysers and hot springs of North Island.

Mount Aspiring National Park
Soaring peaks, alpine lakes, and dense forests make this one of the country's most beautiful national parks.

Fiordland National Park
Fourteen beautiful fjords cut their way through rugged mountain scenery in this remote wilderness. The fjords are home to fur seals, dolphins, and penguins.

Queenstown
One of the biggest tourist resorts in the South Island, Queenstown attracts lovers of extreme sports, such as bungee jumping and white-water rafting.

T a s m a n   S e a

S o u t h e

Livingstone Mountains

La Waka

Queenst

Kepler Mountains

Lake Te Anau

Te Anau

Takitimu Mountains

Hunter Mountains

Kaherekoau Mts

Cameron Mts

Resolution Island

F i o r d l a n d

Te Waewae Bay

Southland
South Island's most southerly region is sparsely populated, with only 2.9 people per sq km (7.4 people per sq mile).

T a s m a n   S e a

Puysegur Point

Milford Sound
This 16-km (10-mile) long fjord is one of the highlights of the Fiordland National Park. The surrounding mountains are very popular with hikers.

Lake Te Anau
With a depth of up to 417 m (1,368 ft), Lake Te Anau contains the largest amount of freshwater in Australasia and Oceania. It is a popular destination for fishing and water sports.

A ROCK SLIDE IN 1991 TOOK 40 M (131 FT) FROM THE

Ruapehu
One of the most active volcanoes in New Zealand, Ruapehu is also a popular ski resort.

ranz Josef Glacier
his glacier descends from the Southern Alps into the lush orests 300 m (984 ft) ove sea level.

Rotorua
The volcanic lake at Rotorua is surrounded by bubbling mud pools and hot springs. The Pohutu Geyser fires hot water 30 m (98.4 ft) into the air.

A l p s

Pegasus Bay

Christchurch

Canterbury Plains

Lake Tekapo

Lake Pukaki

Canterbury Bight

Hawkdun Range

Dumstan Mountains

Kakanui Mountains

Lammerlaw Range

Garvie Mountains

ains

Dunedin

Balclutha

C a t l i n s

Invercargill

The Catlins
This remote region is known for its rugged coastline and rolling, wooded hills.

Toetoes Bay

Invercargill
New Zealand's southernmost city is home to 50,000 people.

Ruapuke Island

Aoraki
New Zealand's highest mountain, Aoraki, is 3,724 m (12,218 ft) high. It is surrounded by eight of the country's largest glaciers.

F o v e a u x   S t r a i t

P A C I F I C

O C E A N

Shelter Point

Codfish Island

Stewart Island

Stewart Island
About 85 per cent of New Zealand's third largest island is set aside as national park. Stewart Island is home to one of the country's biggest populations of kiwis.

Rock islands,
Southern Lagoon, Palau

Spirit house
These long timber buildings are
places in which Melanesian
tribes practise rituals.
They are reserved for men.

Mount Tavurvur,
*New Britain Island,
Papua New Guinea*

Spirit house,
*Sepik River,
Papua New Guinea*

Parliament House,
*Port Moresby,
Papua New Guinea*

Kakadu rock art,
Australia

Cattle stations,
*Barkly Tableland,
Australia*

Kuranda Scenic Railw
*Queensland rainfore.
Australia*

Florence Falls
The forests of Litchfield
National Park are
home to this beautiful
double waterfall.

Florence Falls,
Australia

Bungle Bungle,
*Purnululu National
Park, Australia*

**Karlu Karlu
(Devil's Marbles),**
Northern Territory

Diamantina National Par
Queensland

Wolfe Creek
A meteorite collision
300,000 years ago
left this well-
preserved crater.

**Wolfe Creek
meteor crater,**
Western Australia

Gosses Bluff Crater,
Australia

**Uluru
(Ayers Rock),**
*Northern
Territory*

**Burrup Peninsula
rock art,**
Western Australia

Lake Eyre,
South Australia

**Karijini
National Park,**
Western Australia

**Trans-Australian
Railway,** *Nullarbor
Plain, Australia*

Bunda Cliffs, *Nullarbor Plain,
South Australia*

Adelaide Ov
Adelaide, Austra

Swan Bells,
*Perth, Western
Australia*

○ **Uluru (Ayers Rock)**
This huge mass of sandstone appears to
change colour during the day as the sun
reflects on its different minerals.

Pinnacles Desert,
Western Australia

Fremantle Prison
Built for British convicts
in the 1850s, this prison
is now a tourist site.

Fremantle Prison,
Western Australia

ANZAC Memorial,
Western Australia

N

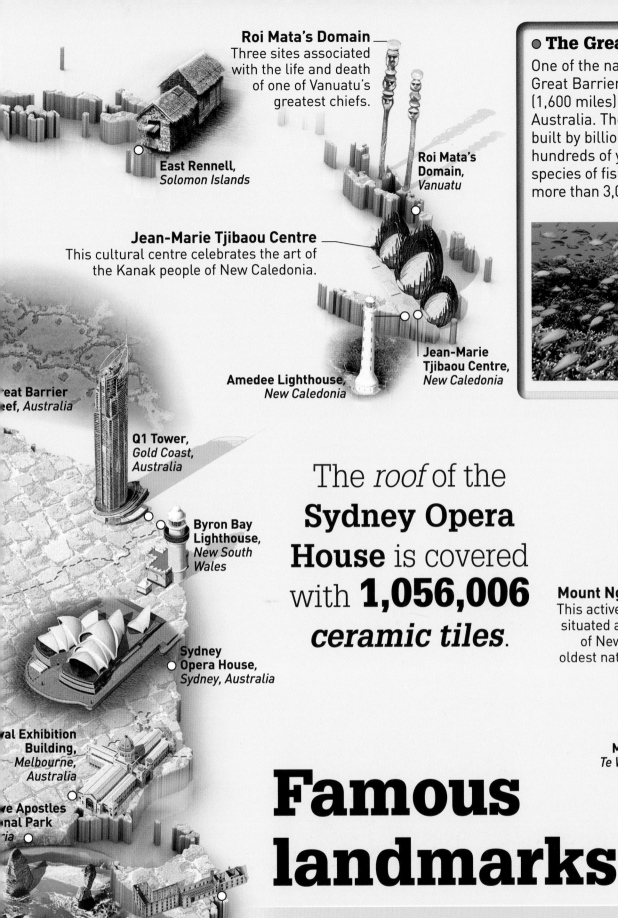

Roi Mata's Domain
Three sites associated with the life and death of one of Vanuatu's greatest chiefs.

East Rennell, *Solomon Islands*

Roi Mata's Domain, *Vanuatu*

Jean-Marie Tjibaou Centre
This cultural centre celebrates the art of the Kanak people of New Caledonia.

Jean-Marie Tjibaou Centre, *New Caledonia*

Amedee Lighthouse, *New Caledonia*

Great Barrier Reef, *Australia*

Q1 Tower, *Gold Coast, Australia*

Byron Bay Lighthouse, *New South Wales*

Sydney Opera House, *Sydney, Australia*

Royal Exhibition Building, *Melbourne, Australia*

Twelve Apostles National Park, Victoria

Port Arthur Historic Site, *Tasmania*

The *roof* of the **Sydney Opera House** is covered with **1,056,006** *ceramic tiles*.

Famous landmarks

The rock formations of the Australian Outback and the dramatic scenery of New Zealand's fjordland are just two of the region's many natural wonders. The region is also home to some iconic modern architecture, such as the Sydney Opera House.

● **The Great Barrier Reef**
One of the natural wonders of the world, the Great Barrier Reef stretches for 2,600 km (1,600 miles) along the northeastern coast of Australia. The reef is made of coral, which is built by billions of tiny creatures over hundreds of years. It is home to about 1,500 species of fish, 14 species of sea snake, and more than 3,000 different types of mollusc.

Sky Tower, *Auckland, New Zealand*

Mount Ngauruhoe,
This active volcano is situated at the heart of New Zealand's oldest national park.

Mount Ngauruhoe, *Tongariro National Park, New Zealand*

Milford Sound, *Te Wahipounamu, New Zealand*

Moeraki Boulders, *Hampden, New Zealand*

Climate

Temperatures soar during the day in the dry interior of Australia, while the coastal regions of the southeast are cooler and wetter. New Zealand has a mild climate, although heavy snow falls during the winter on the South Island. The islands of the Pacific are often hot and humid.

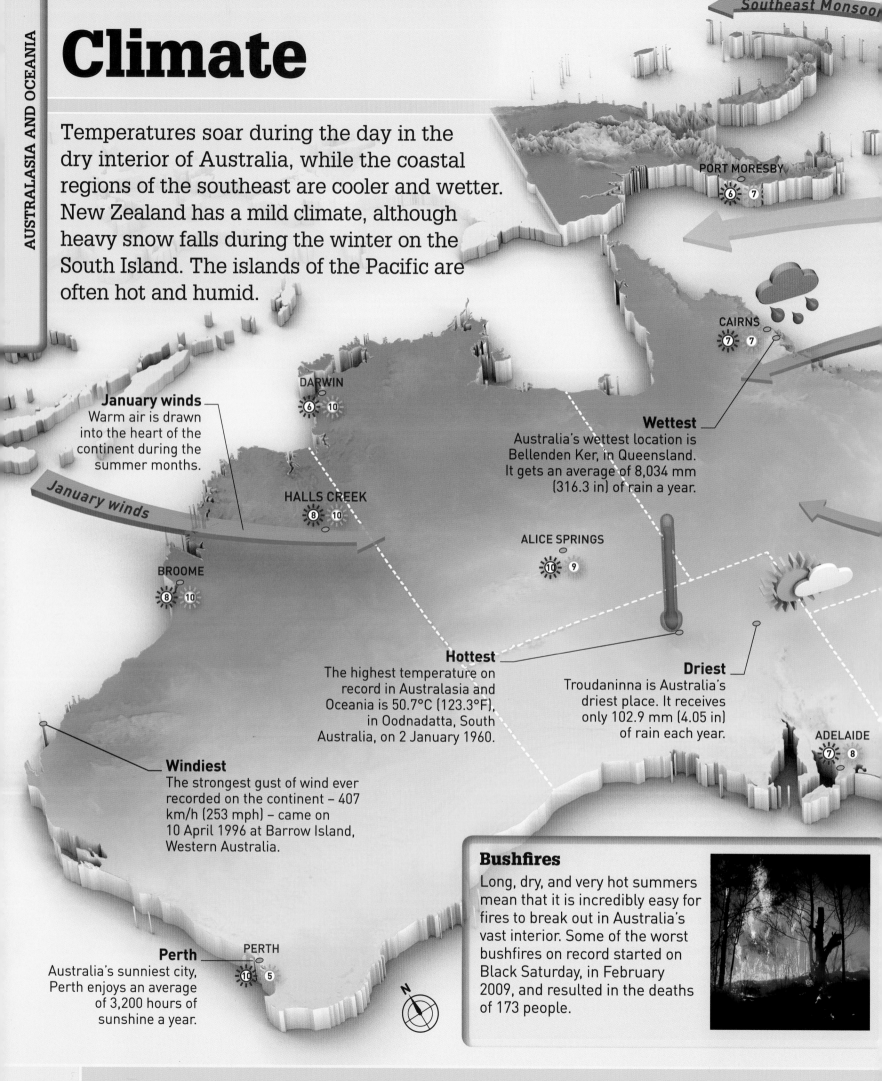

Southeast Monsoon

PORT MORESBY

CAIRNS

DARWIN

January winds
Warm air is drawn into the heart of the continent during the summer months.

January winds

HALLS CREEK

Wettest
Australia's wettest location is Bellenden Ker, in Queensland. It gets an average of 8,034 mm (316.3 in) of rain a year.

ALICE SPRINGS

BROOME

Hottest
The highest temperature on record in Australasia and Oceania is 50.7°C (123.3°F), in Oodnadatta, South Australia, on 2 January 1960.

Driest
Troudaninna is Australia's driest place. It receives only 102.9 mm (4.05 in) of rain each year.

ADELAIDE

Windiest
The strongest gust of wind ever recorded on the continent – 407 km/h (253 mph) – came on 10 April 1996 at Barrow Island, Western Australia.

Bushfires
Long, dry, and very hot summers mean that it is incredibly easy for fires to break out in Australia's vast interior. Some of the worst bushfires on record started on Black Saturday, in February 2009, and resulted in the deaths of 173 people.

Perth
Australia's sunniest city, Perth enjoys an average of 3,200 hours of sunshine a year.

PERTH

IN MAY 2015, THE RESIDENTS OF GOULBURN, NSW, AUSTRALIA, AWOKE

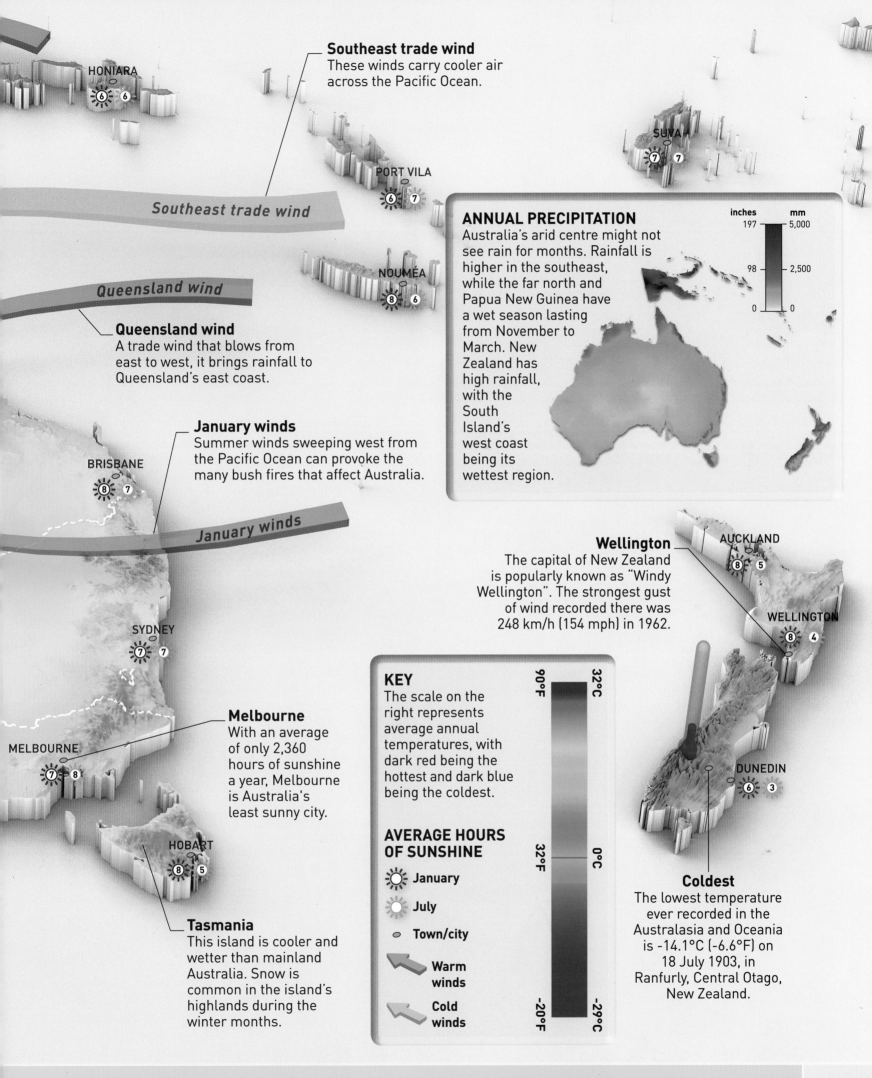

HONIARA 6 6

Southeast trade wind
These winds carry cooler air
across the Pacific Ocean.

SUVA 7 7

PORT VILA 6 7

Southeast trade wind

Queensland wind

NOUMÉA 8 6

ANNUAL PRECIPITATION
Australia's arid centre might not
see rain for months. Rainfall is
higher in the southeast,
while the far north and
Papua New Guinea have
a wet season lasting
from November to
March. New
Zealand has
high rainfall,
with the
South
Island's
west coast
being its
wettest region.

inches | mm
197 | 5,000
98 | 2,500
0 | 0

Queensland wind
A trade wind that blows from
east to west, it brings rainfall to
Queensland's east coast.

January winds
Summer winds sweeping west from
the Pacific Ocean can provoke the
many bush fires that affect Australia.

BRISBANE 8 7

January winds

Wellington
The capital of New Zealand
is popularly known as "Windy
Wellington". The strongest gust
of wind recorded there was
248 km/h (154 mph) in 1962.

AUCKLAND 8 5

WELLINGTON 8 4

SYDNEY 7 7

Melbourne
With an average
of only 2,360
hours of sunshine
a year, Melbourne
is Australia's
least sunny city.

MELBOURNE 7 8

KEY
The scale on the
right represents
average annual
temperatures, with
dark red being the
hottest and dark blue
being the coldest.

90°F | 32°C
32°F | 0°C
-20°F | -29°C

**AVERAGE HOURS
OF SUNSHINE**

☼ January

☀ July

◦ Town/city

➤ Warm winds

➤ Cold winds

DUNEDIN 6 3

HOBART 8 5

Coldest
The lowest temperature
ever recorded in the
Australasia and Oceania
is -14.1°C (-6.6°F) on
18 July 1903, in
Ranfurly, Central Otago,
New Zealand.

Tasmania
This island is cooler and
wetter than mainland
Australia. Snow is
common in the island's
highlands during the
winter months.

TO FIND THOUSANDS OF SPIDERS HAD RAINED ONTO THEIR TOWN.

BIOMES

Deserts and temperate broadleaf forest are dominant in Australia, while the mountain habitat of the Southern Alps dominates New Zealand.

- Temperate broadleaf forest
- Temperate grassland
- Mediterranean
- Tropical broadleaf forest
- Tropical dry broadleaf forest
- Tropical/sub-tropical grassland
- Mountain
- Desert
- Mangrove

Sir David's echidna
This spiny anteater, named for British naturalist Sir David Attenborough, is critically endangered.

Southern cassowary
Its horn-like crest helps this bird push head-first through vegetation.

Queen Alexandra birdwing butterfly
The world's largest butterfly, it has a wingspan of up to 31 cm (12 in).

Cuscus
This possum uses its strong tail to climb through trees.

Clownfish
This fish hides amo the poisonous tentacles of sea anemo

Saltwater crocodile
The largest of the reptiles, this crocodile drowns its prey by rolling it in the water.

Frilled lizard
When threatened, this lizard opens a flap of skin to warn off predators.

Black flying fox
This fruit bat's wingspan reaches up to 2 m (6.6 ft).

Cockatoo
These noisy parrots gather in flocks that can include several hundred birds.

Dingo
Descended from prehistoric domestic dogs, dingoes are widespread throughout Australia.

Blue-spotted stingray
Hiding patiently on the seabed, this ray ambushes passing snails and crabs.

Walla
Like their larg cousin, the kangaro wallabies carry the young in pouche

Kangaroo
These animals are marsupials, meaning that females nurture their young in pouches.

Spiny anteater
One of the few mammals to lay eggs, the spiny anteater is protected by sharp spines.

Wombat
This marsupial lives in complex burrows that can be up to 200 m (660 ft) long.

Dwarf bearded dragon
This small lizard lives off insects, invertebrates, and small mammals.

Inland taipan
The most venomou land snake in the world, its prey includes rats and oth small mammals.

Western brown snake
This fast-moving snake preys on mice and lizards.

Redback spider
A bite from this spider can cause pain, sickness, and convulsions.

Emu
Australia's largest bird can reach up to 1.9 m (6.2 ft) in height. Its shaggy plumage resembles hair.

Tiger snake
This extremely venomous snake preys on frogs, lizards, birds, and small mammals.

Numbat
This marsupial rips open termite nests with its powerful front teeth and claws.

Poisonous snakes

Some of the world's most dangerous snakes live in Australia. The eastern brown snake causes the most deaths, followed by the western brown snake, and the tiger snake.

The eastern brown snake can be extremely aggressive.

AUSTRALIA IS HOME TO AROUND 300,000 WILD CAMELS - DESCENDANTS

Fijian monkey-faced bat
This bat can only be found on Fiji, but is endangered due to habitat loss.

Coconut crab
The largest land-living crab in the world uses its pincers to pierce coconut shells.

Banded sea krait
The coral reef provides a hunting ground for this highly venomous sea snake.

Giant manta ray
To feed, this ray pulls in water through its mouth, collecting up to 30 kg (66 lb) of plankton each day.

The *platypus* has a pair of **venomous spurs** on its hind legs.

Koala
Eucalyptus leaves provide the koala with its staple diet.

Green turtle
This turtle feeds on seagrasses and is found throughout the region's seas.

Kiwi
This nocturnal, flightless bird preys on earthworms and other invertebrates.

Regent bowerbird
The male's plumage is glossy black and gold, while the female's is drab olive-brown.

Dusky dolphin
Highly acrobatic, these dolphins can be found in the coastal waters around New Zealand.

Lyrebird
During courtship, the male displays an extraordinary repertoire of songs.

Kakapo
This large, flightless parrot lives off seeds and fruit.

Duck-billed platypus
With its webbed feet and paddle-like tail, the platypus is well equipped for its semi-aquatic life.

New Zealand sea lion
This highly endangered sea lion preys on crabs and penguins in the seas around New Zealand's South Island.

...ookaburra
...nown for its ...ughing call, ...kookaburra ...ts mice and ...all reptiles.

Tasmanian devil
The size of a small dog, this ferocious marsupial feeds on animal carcasses.

Wildlife

Australia and New Zealand are home to some weird and wonderful animals, among them egg-laying mammals, marsupials, and flightless birds. The seas of Oceania, meanwhile, are home to turtles, dolphins, and an extraordinary range of tropical fish.

Fijian monkey-faced bat
This bat can only be found on Fiji, but is endangered due to habitat loss.

Coconut crab
The largest land-living crab in the world uses its pincers to pierce coconut shells.

Banded sea krait
The coral reef provides a hunting ground for this highly venomous sea snake.

The *platypus* has a pair of **venomous spurs** on its hind legs.

Giant manta ray
To feed, this ray pulls in water through its mouth, collecting up to 30 kg (66 lb) of plankton each day.

Green turtle
This turtle feeds on seagrasses and is found throughout the region's seas.

Kiwi
This nocturnal, flightless bird preys on earthworms and other invertebrates.

Koala
Eucalyptus leaves provide the koala with its staple diet.

Regent bowerbird
The male's plumage is glossy black and gold, while the female's is drab olive-brown.

Dusky dolphin
Highly acrobatic, these dolphins can be found in the coastal waters around New Zealand.

Lyrebird
During courtship, the male displays an extraordinary repertoire of songs.

Kakapo
This large, flightless parrot lives off seeds and fruit.

Duck-billed platypus
With its webbed feet and paddle-like tail, the platypus is well equipped for its semi-aquatic life.

New Zealand sea lion
This highly endangered sea lion preys on crabs and penguins in the seas around New Zealand's South Island.

kookaburra
nown for its ughing call, kookaburra ts mice and all reptiles.

Tasmanian devil
The size of a small dog, this ferocious marsupial feeds on animal carcasses.

Wildlife

Australia and New Zealand are home to some weird and wonderful animals, among them egg-laying mammals, marsupials, and flightless birds. The seas of Oceania, meanwhile, are home to turtles, dolphins, and an extraordinary range of tropical fish.

POLAR REGIONS

Extreme cold
The North and South Poles are the northernmost and southernmost points on Earth. The climate there is extremely harsh, with temperatures rarely rising above 0°C (32°F).

South Pole Station
The Amundsen-Scott research station is located at the Geographical South Pole. First opened in 1956, it can house up to 200 researchers.

Southern elephant seal
The largest of all seals, males can be over 6 m (20 ft) long and weigh up to 4,000 kg (8,800 lb).

Vinson Massif
Part of a large mountain range by the Ronne Ice Shelf, this massif contains Antarctica's highest peak, Mount Vinson, at 4,892 m (16,050 ft).

Antarctic minke whale
This small whale lives in groups of two to four.

Antarctic ice fish
A type of anti-freeze in its blood enables this fish to survive in ice-cold water.

Wandering albatross
With the largest wing span of any bird – up to 3.5 m (11.5 ft) – it spends most of its life in flight at sea.

Snowy sheathbill
This bird does not swim, so steals fish, and eggs or chicks, from penguins.

South polar skua
Up to 53 cm (21 in) tall, this large bird breeds in Antarctica before returning to a life on the oceans.

Antarctic toothfish
Growing up to 1.7 m (5.6 ft) long, this fish feeds on squid, crabs, prawns, and smaller fish.

Leopard seal
This fierce, sharp-toothed predator hunts other seals, penguins, and fish.

Antarctica

Earth's southernmost continent is the coldest region in the world, with temperatures reaching as low as -93.2°C (-135.8°F). Despite the harsh conditions, the continent is home to a number of animals. However, climate change is a threat to both Antarctica's animals and landscape.

Ross Ice Shelf
This enormous layer of floating ice is over 600 km (370 miles) long. About 90 per cent of its ice lies underwater.

Killer whale
In fact the largest of all dolphins, this is one of the world's most powerful predators.

Colossal squid
This squid is up to 14 m (46 ft) long, and has sharp hooks on its limbs.

Antarctic fur seal
Males battle for territory during the breeding season when these seals gather in vast numbers on land.

Adelie penguin
Parents take turns in feeding and keeping their eggs safe from predators.

Geographical South Pole
This is Earth's southernmost point. The Ceremonial South Pole, situated 180 m (590 ft) from the Geographical South Pole, is marked by a pole surrounded by the flags of the nations that signed the Antarctic Treaty, an agreement that set aside the continent for scientific research.

Extreme climate
The average annual temperature in Antarctica is around -50°C (-58°F). Winds often reach storm force, there is little snowfall, and the sun does not rise at all between March and September.

Emperor penguin
The largest of all penguins has an average height of 115 cm (45 in). They can survive in temperatures as low as -60° C (-76° F).

Gentoo penguin
These speedy swimmers have red beaks, white feather caps, and orange feet.

KEY
Antarctica is a cold desert. Where it is not covered in ice, the barren ground is gravel or rock.

☐ Ice
☐ Tundra

Mount Erebus
One of the world's most active volcanoes and, at 3,794 m (12,448 ft), the highest active volcano in Antarctica, Mount Erebus has a very rare, bubbling, lava lake.

Snow petrel
These birds nest on cliffs, but prefer to gather on pack ice.

IT MELTED, WORLD SEA LEVELS WOULD RISE BY ABOUT 60 M (200 FT).

Bowhead whale
These whales can break through ice to breathe and can live for up to 130 years.

North Pole
Earth's northernmost point is situated on an ice cap. Below it, the Arctic Ocean is around 4,200 m (13,800 ft) deep.

Siberian salamander
This amphibian can survive in very low temperatures by deep-freezing itself until temperatures start to rise.

Arctic hare
These hares do not hibernate, and find food under the snow.

Bewick's swan
Each individual swan has a unique pattern on its black and yellow beak.

Arctic skua
These aggressive seabirds steal food from other birds by attacking them in mid-air.

Guillemot
Found throughout the Arctic, these birds can dive as deep as 60 m (197 ft) to find food.

Rock ptarmiga
This bird change its white feather to speckled brow in summer.

Spectacled eider
After breeding on the coasts of Alaska and northeast Siberia, these ducks gather in spots of open sea in the pack ice.

Arctic tern
These small birds fly 70,000 km (43,496 miles) between the North and South Poles every year.

BIOMES
- Ice
- Tundra
- Boreal forest/taiga

Lake Hazen
One of the largest lakes in the Arctic region, the 269-m (883-ft) deep Lake Hazen, in Canada, is frozen over for most of the year.

Greenland sha
A slow-swimmi scavenger, this sha sniffs out de animals in the wat

THE ARCTIC SEA ICE IS UP TO 4 M (13 FT) THICK; THE AREA

Yenisei
The Yenisei river, in [R]ussia, is the largest river [to] flow out into the Arctic [O]cean. Its 50-km (31-mile) [w]ide estuary is frozen for [lo]ng parts of the year.

Unlike Antarctica, the Arctic is not a continent, but the area of frozen waters surrounding the North Pole. It includes the northernmost parts of three continents – North America, Europe, and Asia. Many different animals have made a home in this inhospitable region.

Siberian crane
This bird easily snips off roots and catches fish with its saw-edged beak.

Ermine
This mammal's coat turns from brown to white in winter for camouflage.

[B]eluga whale
[W]hite in colour, [this] small whale [spe]aks in clicks [a]nd whistles.

Porbeagle shark
This shark grows up to 2.5 m (8.2 ft) in length and feeds on squid and fish.

Spiny dogfish
This fish is one of the most numerous species of shark in the world.

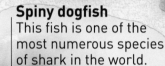

Lemming
Soft, warm fur helps this rodent stay active through the winter.

Brent goose
Unlike other geese, the Brent flies in long lines instead of in a V-shape.

Narwhal
The tusks of this small whale can grow up to 3 m (9.8 ft).

Polar bear
A powerful predator, this bear roams over land and pack ice to find prey.

Bluntnose sixgill shark
This fast-swimming shark has six gills instead of the five normal in most sharks.

Puffin
60 per cent of the world's puffins live in Iceland.

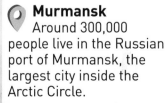

Murmansk
Around 300,000 people live in the Russian port of Murmansk, the largest city inside the Arctic Circle.

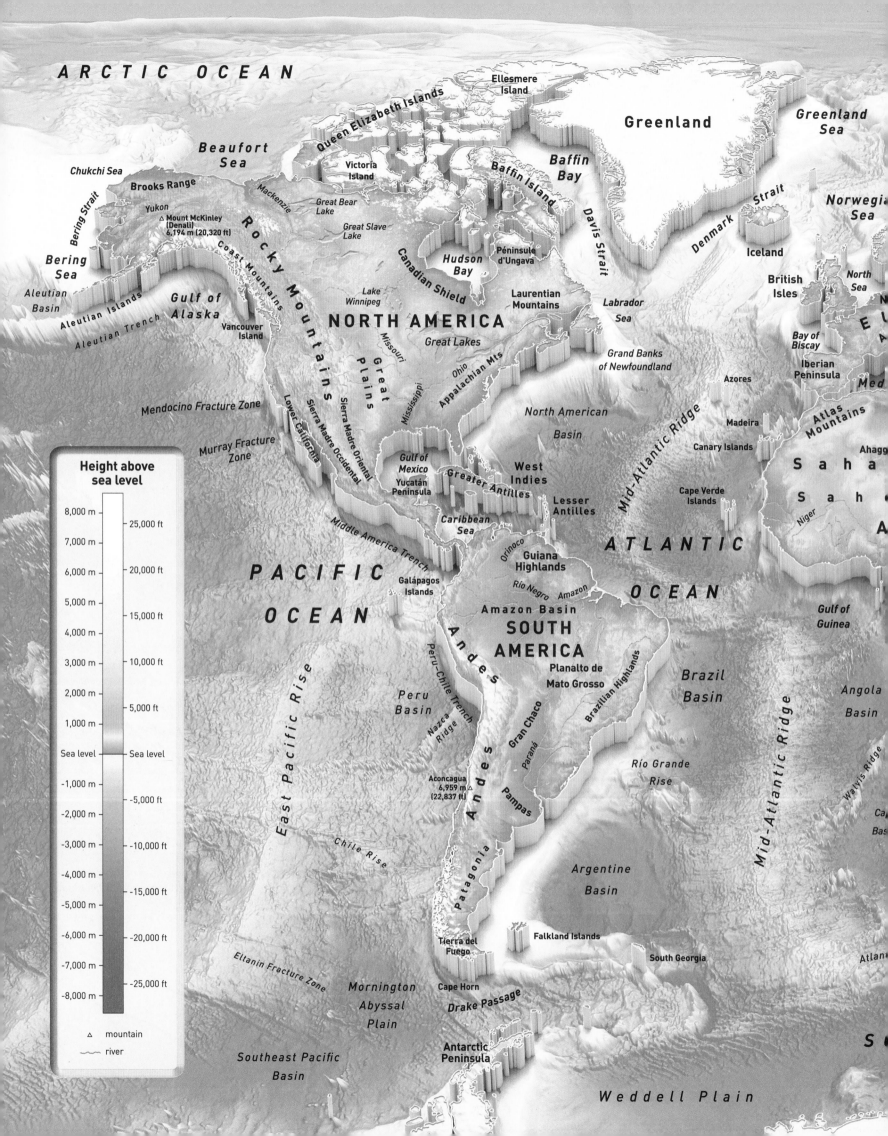

ARCTIC OCEAN

Chukchi Sea

Beaufort Sea

Queen Elizabeth Islands

Ellesmere Island

Greenland

Greenland Sea

Victoria Island

Baffin Island

Baffin Bay

Bering Strait

Brooks Range

Yukon

△ Mount McKinley (Denali) 6,194 m (20,320 ft)

Mackenzie

Great Bear Lake

Denmark Strait

Norwegian Sea

Bering Sea

Coast Mountains

Great Slave Lake

Péninsule d'Ungava

Davis Strait

Iceland

Aleutian Basin

Gulf of Alaska

Rocky Mountains

Canadian Shield

Hudson Bay

Laurentian Mountains

Labrador Sea

British Isles

North Sea

Aleutian Islands

Lake Winnipeg

NORTH AMERICA

Grand Banks of Newfoundland

Bay of Biscay

Aleutian Trench

Vancouver Island

Missouri

Great Lakes

Azores

Iberian Peninsula

EU

Mendocino Fracture Zone

Great Plains

Ohio

Appalachian Mts

North American Basin

Madeira

Atlas Mountains

Murray Fracture Zone

Lower California

Sierra Madre Oriental

Sierra Madre Occidental

Mississippi

Canary Islands

Sahar

Sah

Gulf of Mexico

Yucatán Peninsula

Greater Antilles

West Indies

Mid-Atlantic Ridge

Cape Verde Islands

Ahagg

PACIFIC OCEAN

Middle America Trench

Caribbean Sea

Lesser Antilles

ATLANTIC OCEAN

Niger

A

Galápagos Islands

Orinoco

Guiana Highlands

Río Negro   Amazon

Gulf of Guinea

Peru Basin

Amazon Basin

SOUTH AMERICA

East Pacific Rise

Andes

Peru-Chile Trench

Planalto de Mato Grosso

Brazilian Highlands

Brazil Basin

Angola Basin

Nazca Ridge

Gran Chaco

Aconcagua 6,959 m △ (22,837 ft)

Paraná

Pampas

Río Grande Rise

Mid-Atlantic Ridge

Watvis Ridge

Chile Rise

Patagonia

Argentine Basin

Cap

Bas

Eltanin Fracture Zone

Tierra del Fuego

Cape Horn

Falkland Islands

South Georgia

Atlan

Drake Passage

Mornington Abyssal Plain

Southeast Pacific Basin

Antarctic Peninsula

Weddell Plain

S

Height above sea level

8,000 m	25,000 ft
7,000 m	20,000 ft
6,000 m	
5,000 m	15,000 ft
4,000 m	10,000 ft
3,000 m	
2,000 m	5,000 ft
1,000 m	
Sea level	Sea level
-1,000 m	-5,000 ft
-2,000 m	-10,000 ft
-3,000 m	
-4,000 m	-15,000 ft
-5,000 m	-20,000 ft
-6,000 m	
-7,000 m	-25,000 ft
-8,000 m	

△ mountain

river

INLAND
Helsinki
ESTONIA
LATVIA
nuis LITHUANIA • Moscow
Minsk
BELARUS
Kiev
AKIA UKRAINE
est MOLDOVA
Chisinau
A ROMANIA
grade Bucharest
Sofia BULGARIA
Pristina
Ankara
ECE Skopje
GEORGIA Tbilisi
Nicosia ARMENIA AZERBAIJAN
CYPRUS Yerevan Baku
LEBANON SYRIA
ISRAEL Damascus
Jerusalem Amman Baghdad
IRAQ
Cairo JORDAN KUWAIT
Kuwait
BAHRAIN
EGYPT Riyadh Manama QATAR
SAUDI Doha
ARABIA Abu Dhabi
UAE Muscat

RUSSIAN FEDERATION

Astana

KAZAKHSTAN

UZBEKISTAN
Tashkent Bishkek
Asgabat TURKMENISTAN KYRGYZSTAN
TAJIKISTAN
Dushanbe
Tehran
Kabul
AFGHANISTAN Islamabad
IRAN
PAKISTAN New Delhi NEPAL
Kathmandu
Thimphu
BHUTAN
BANGLADESH
Dhaka

MONGOLIA
Ulan Bator

CHINA

Beijing

NORTH
KOREA
Pyongyang
Seoul JAPAN
SOUTH Sejong City
KOREA Tokyo

Midway
Islands
(US)

SUDAN
Khartoum
ERITREA
Asmara Sana
Sana YEMEN OMAN
DJIBOUTI
Djibouti
Addis Ababa
SOUTH
REPUBLIC SUDAN
ETHIOPIA
Juba
SOMALIA
UGANDA
Kampala KENYA
Kigali Nairobi
M. REP. RWANDA
Bujumbura
ONGO BURUNDI Dodoma
TANZANIA

BURMA
(MYANMAR)
Nay Pyi Taw
Vientiane LAOS
THAILAND
Bangkok CAMBODIA
Phnom Penh

Hanoi VIETNAM

Taipei
TAIWAN

Manila

PHILIPPINES

Wake Island (US)

Northern
Mariana
Islands
(US)

Guam
(US)

MARSHALL ISLANDS

INDIA

SRI LANKA
Colombo
Sri Jayewardenapura
Kotte

Andaman
Islands
(India)

Laccadive Islands
(India)

Nicobar
Islands
(India)

BRUNEI
Bandar Seri Begawan

PALAU
Ngerulmud

MICRONESIA • Palikir

Baker &
Howland Islands
(US)

MALDIVES Male

MALAYSIA
Kuala Lumpur
Putrajaya
SINGAPORE
Singapore

NAURU
Bairiki
KIRIBATI

British Indian
Ocean Territory
(UK)

Jakarta I N D O N E S I A

PAPUA NEW GUINEA

SOLOMON
ISLANDS
Port Moresby Honiara

TUVALU
Fongafale

Tokelau
(NZ) Apia

SEYCHELLES

Victoria

COMOROS
Moroni

Mayotte
(France)
Antananarivo

MAURITIUS
Port Louis

Réunion
(France)

ZAMBIA MALAWI
Lusaka Lilongwe
Harare
MOZAMBIQUE
ZIMBABWE
MADAGASCAR
TSWANA
orone Pretoria
Mbabane Maputo
SWAZILAND
fontein LESOTHO
Maseru
UTH
RICA

Christmas Island
(Australia)

Cocos (Keeling) Island
(Australia)

Ashmore & Cartier Islands
(Australia)

Dili EAST
TIMOR

WESTERN
AUSTRALIA

NORTHERN
TERRITORY

QUEENSLAND

Coral Sea
Islands
(Australia)

New
Caledonia
(France)

VANUATU
Port-Vila

Suva
FIJI

Wallis
& Futuna
(France) SAMOA

TONGA
Nuku'alofa

Amsterdam Island
(France)

St-Paul Island
(France)

SOUTH
AUSTRALIA

NEW SOUTH
WALES

AUSTRALIA

Norfolk Island
(Australia)

Kermadec Islands
(New Zealand)

Prince Edward
Islands
(South Africa)

Crozet Islands
(France)

Kerguelen
(France)

Canberra VICTORIA
AUSTRALIAN
CAPITAL
TERRITORY

TASMANIA

NEW ZEALAND
Wellington

Chatham Islands
(New Zealand)

Bounty Islands
(New Zealand)

Auckland Islands
(New Zealand)

Macquarie Island
(Australia)

Country abbreviations

BEL.	Belgium
BOS. & HERZ.	Bosnia and Herzegovina
CZECH REP.	Czech Republic
KOS.	Kosovo
LIECH.	Liechtenstein
LUX.	Luxembourg
MAC.	Macedonia
MON.	Montenegro
NETH.	Netherlands
NZ	New Zealand
RUSS. FED.	Russian Federation
SM	San Marino
SLVN.	Slovenia
SWITZ.	Switzerland
UAE	United Arab Emirates
UK	United Kingdom
US	United States of America
VAT. CITY	Vatican City

A N T A R C T I C A